Contents

Icons and features

Make the Link   **Key Concept**   **Top Tips**

Preparing for Higher Business Management

About this Success Guide

This *Success Guide* is structured around the three units of the Higher Business Management course and breaks down the course content into small manageable topics for you to revise. There are regular **Quick Tests** for you to complete and **Top Tips** for you to read and take note of. The section on **tracking your learning journey** will enable you to manage your revision in an organised and helpful way. This revision book is designed to give you the **essential** knowledge to help you prepare for your SQA examination and the end of unit assessments (NABs) that you will have to pass to achieve the award of Higher Business Management.

It is very important that you note down anything you do not understand and ask your teacher or lecturer for help. **Do not** move on to the next topic until you fully understand the previous one. Please remember that any Higher course requires a lot of hard work and this course is no exception. Plan your revision very carefully and do as much work (and past papers!) as you can.

Top Tip

Managing your time in NABs and examinations is crucial!

The course

This course is extremely interesting and varied and is structured around three units as shown below. It builds upon any previous study of Business Management and is a useful qualification to have no matter what you intend to do after school or college.

Unit 1	Business Enterprise	This unit provides you with a knowledge of the role of business in contemporary society. It will develop your understanding of the role, purpose and decision making processes and the use of Information and Communications Technology (ICT) in today's business environment.
Unit 2	BDA: Marketing and Operations	This unit requires you to analyse the roles of the marketing and operations in organisations. It will enable you to analyse the marketing and operations decisions that organisations make.
Unit 3	BDA: Finance and Human Resource Management	This unit requires you to analyse the roles of the finance and human resources functions in organisations. It requires you to analyse the finance and human resources decisions that organisations make.

Note – BDA stands for Business Decision Areas.

Unit and course assessment

To pass the course, you must undertake two types of assessment: unit and course assessment.

Unit assessment

You have three unit assessments to complete, one for each unit of the course. These unit assessments are known as 'NABs' and are set by the SQA but marked by your teacher/lecturer. (They are known as internal assessments.) You will be given one hour to complete each NAB and **must** achieve 50% of the available marks to pass. If you do not pass the first time, you will usually be given one further opportunity to reach the standard required. ➡

Success guides

HIGHER
Business Management

✕ Lee Coutts ✕

Contents

Course assessment

Course assessment is made up of an examination paper which you sit at the end of the course. This exam is set and marked by the SQA and is used to grade candidates A, B, C, D or no award. (It is known as the external assessment.) To achieve a C grade, you usually need to obtain around 50% of the available marks. The exam is of 2 hours 30 minutes duration and marked out of 100. It comprises two sections, each worth 50 marks.

Top Tip

Knowing how to present your answer to the first question in Section 1 is crucial.

- Section 1 consists of a case study which you will need to read and then answer questions on. Question 1 in this section always asks you to **identify problems** in the case study with **reference to particular areas of the course**. Use these areas as headings and **write down the problems identified from the case under the appropriate heading**. The question will tell you which areas of the course you need to focus on in your answer and these vary each year. This is an easy question to do well on if you know how to answer it (practise!).
- Section 2 consists of five questions, each with several parts, and you need to answer any two. Read all five questions carefully before deciding which two to answer.

Sample examination questions are provided in this *Success Guide* for you to try. These have been taken directly from past SQA examination papers. Use all of your notes to help you answer these. Leckie & Leckie's *Higher Business Management Grade Booster* and *Higher Business Management Practice Papers for SQA Exams* provide excellent advice on unit and course assessment, including examples for you to work through.

Command words

Command words are instructions to **you** (not your teacher!) on how to write, structure and present your answer. It is very important that **you** know what the command word is asking you to do. For example, an **identify** question requires a completely different answer from a **describe** question. You must follow the command word(s) given in each question or you will not achieve full marks for that question. You must also remember to look at the marks available for each question and use this as a guide to the length of answer you need to write. The command words that are used by the SQA for Higher Business Management are:

Command word	Definition
Compare	Identify similarities and differences between two or more factors.
Describe	Provide a thorough description.
Discuss	Examine closely taking account of strengths and weaknesses in an argument; offer reasons for and against.
Distinguish	Identify the differences between two or more factors.
Explain	Give a detailed response (definition **and** explanation) as to how/why something may benefit/hinder.
Identify	Give the name or identifying characteristics of something.
Justify	Give reasons to support suggestions, conclusions.
Outline	State the main features.

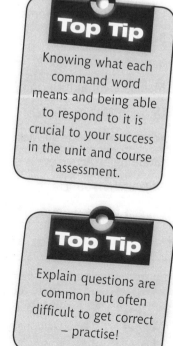

Top Tip

Knowing what each command word means and being able to respond to it is crucial to your success in the unit and course assessment.

Top Tip

Explain questions are common but often difficult to get correct – practise!

Tracking Your Learning Journey

Now that you know how the course is structured and will be assessed, you can get on with learning what you need to learn! This section on tracking your learning journey will enable you to keep check on your progress and record any area that is causing you concern. It has been designed for you to use when preparing for your NABs, preliminary examination and your SQA examination.

Listed below are the different topic areas as defined by the SQA that you need to learn; they are also the page headings used in this book. When your NABs, preliminary examination and SQA examination are approaching, you should rate yourself on how confident you are on each topic. You should base what you know on evidence – eg the feedback you have from your teacher, results of homework exercises and from attempting past paper questions on that particular topic. The rating system given is based on a set of traffic lights: **green** means you understand the topic fully, **amber** means you have an understanding of the main points but there are gaps in your knowledge and **red** means you have no or only a little knowledge of that topic. Where you are unsure of something, the page numbers you should refer to in this guide are given so you know exactly where to look for the information. **There are no excuses for not knowing something!**

UNIT 1	Knowledge for NAB	Knowledge for Prelim	Knowledge for SQA Exam	Page Number
Role of Business in Contemporary Society	■ ■ ■	■ ■ ■	■ ■ ■	8
Types of Business Organisations	■ ■ ■	■ ■ ■	■ ■ ■	10
Objectives	■ ■ ■	■ ■ ■	■ ■ ■	14
Stakeholders	■ ■ ■	■ ■ ■	■ ■ ■	16
Factors affecting Business Activity	■ ■ ■	■ ■ ■	■ ■ ■	18
Growth	■ ■ ■	■ ■ ■	■ ■ ■	20
Business as a Dynamic Activity	■ ■ ■	■ ■ ■	■ ■ ■	22
Sources and Types of Information	■ ■ ■	■ ■ ■	■ ■ ■	24
Uses and Value of Information	■ ■ ■	■ ■ ■	■ ■ ■	26
Business and ICT	■ ■ ■	■ ■ ■	■ ■ ■	28
Benefits and Costs of ICT	■ ■ ■	■ ■ ■	■ ■ ■	30
Management and Decision Making	■ ■ ■	■ ■ ■	■ ■ ■	32
Decision Making Models	■ ■ ■	■ ■ ■	■ ■ ■	34
What Makes Decision Making Difficult?	■ ■ ■	■ ■ ■	■ ■ ■	36
Grouping of Activities	■ ■ ■	■ ■ ■	■ ■ ■	38
Organisation Structures	■ ■ ■	■ ■ ■	■ ■ ■	42
Aspects of Organisation Structure	■ ■ ■	■ ■ ■	■ ■ ■	44

NAB RESULT ____/40   DATE_____

There are lots of words and key terms to be learned on this course. We have helped you by providing a list of Key Concepts at the end of each chapter. You should keep a 'Business Dictionary' and write down all of the Key Concepts and their definitions you come across in this *Success Guide*. **Your written work will be much better if you can use appropriate business terminology!**

UNIT 2

	Knowledge for NAB	Knowledge for Prelim	Knowledge for SQA Exam	Page Number
What is Marketing?	▪▪▪	▪▪▪	▪▪▪	46
Product	▪▪▪	▪▪▪	▪▪▪	48
Price	▪▪▪	▪▪▪	▪▪▪	50
Place	▪▪▪	▪▪▪	▪▪▪	52
Promotion	▪▪▪	▪▪▪	▪▪▪	56
Market Research	▪▪▪	▪▪▪	▪▪▪	60
Role and Importance of Operations	▪▪▪	▪▪▪	▪▪▪	64
Managing Stock, Warehouses and Distribution	▪▪▪	▪▪▪	▪▪▪	68
Production Methods	▪▪▪	▪▪▪	▪▪▪	72
Managing Quality	▪▪▪	▪▪▪	▪▪▪	74

NAB RESULT _____/40 **DATE**_____

UNIT 3

	Knowledge for NAB	Knowledge for Prelim	Knowledge for SQA Exam	Page Number
Organisations and Finance	▪▪▪	▪▪▪	▪▪▪	78
Final Accounts	▪▪▪	▪▪▪	▪▪▪	80
Cash Flow Management	▪▪▪	▪▪▪	▪▪▪	82
Using Financial Information	▪▪▪	▪▪▪	▪▪▪	84
Ratio Analysis	▪▪▪	▪▪▪	▪▪▪	86
Sources of Finance	▪▪▪	▪▪▪	▪▪▪	90
Human Resources and Changing Employment Patterns	▪▪▪	▪▪▪	▪▪▪	92
Recruitment	▪▪▪	▪▪▪	▪▪▪	96
Selection	▪▪▪	▪▪▪	▪▪▪	98
Training and Development	▪▪▪	▪▪▪	▪▪▪	102
Employee Relations	▪▪▪	▪▪▪	▪▪▪	104
Law and the Workplace	▪▪▪	▪▪▪	▪▪▪	106

NAB RESULT _____/40 **DATE**_____

Preliminary Examination Result   Mark _____   % Grade _____   Date _____

Once you have done your preliminary examination and have your result, you will be in a good position to make a list of actions you need to take to help improve your final examination result. You should record these in the table below.

Action Number	What action I need to take to improve my final result	Date completed
1		
2		
3		

Please do not underestimate the effort and work you need to put in to do well. Remember – there is only one mark between each grade and the more work you put in, the greater chance of getting a high grade.

Role of Business in Contemporary Society

Enterprise and entrepreneurs

Entrepreneurs are people who think of an idea for a business and develop it. They will combine different resources (inputs) to provide a good or service (output). Their role is different from that of a manager. Entrepreneurs can identify opportunities and combine the resources needed to make it a success. They have certain characteristics or features:

- They are willing to take risks.
- They are known and associated with innovation.
- They combine the factors of production.
- They use their initiative to make decisions and solve problems.

There are many famous examples of entrepreneurs including Richard Branson (Virgin Group), Bill Gates (Microsoft) and Duncan Bannatyne (Bannatyne's Health club).

> Between the role of entrepreneur and the role of a manager.

Wealth creation

Entrepreneurs combine the four **factors of production** in order to produce goods and services that people want. Factors of production are the resources required to produce a good or provide a service.

Factor of Production	Description
Land	The natural resources of the world, eg water, fields and trees.
Labour	The workforce (human labour).
Capital	The equipment, machinery and tools used by a business. The money that the owner has invested is also included.
Enterprise	The person (entrepreneur) who combines all of the factors of production to produce a good or service.

Top Tip

Make sure you understand what is meant by the terms 'adding value' and 'creating wealth'.

At every stage of the production process, **value** is added and therefore more **wealth** is created. This is because something happens (eg a part or an ingredient added) at each stage when the good or service is being produced.

Production, consumption, needs and wants

Production refers to the making of goods to be sold or to move on to another stage of production.
Consumption refers to the purchasing of goods or services.

Needs are essential for survival, ie water, food and shelter.

Wants are what people demand after their needs have been satisfied.

People buy goods and services to meet their basic needs and then to satisfy their wants. Someone with limited money to spend would ensure that they buy the basic items they require (eg food, water) before purchasing something that is not essential for survival (eg a computer game).

Sectors of industry

Based on the good produced or service they provide, businesses can be grouped into sectors of industry. Some businesses may belong to more than one sector.

Sector of industry	Description
Primary	Businesses in this sector extract materials from the ground. *Examples – fishing, farming and coal mining.*
Secondary	Businesses in this sector are involved in the manufacturing (making) of products. *Examples – cars, computers and cakes.*
Tertiary	Businesses in this sector provide a service. *Examples – supermarkets, airlines and accountants.*

Top Tip

Use examples where you can to support your answers.

The United Kingdom's secondary sector has decreased in size in recent years. This is because of:
- increased competition from abroad, where things can be produced more cheaply
- changes in consumer demand
- changes in and the introduction of new government policy and laws.

There has been a growth in the tertiary sector and the number of people employed in jobs in this sector has increased significantly.

Sample examination questions

1. Describe the role of an entrepreneur in a business. (4 marks)

Quick Test 1

1. Explain what is meant by an entrepreneur.
2. Identify and describe the four factors of production.
3. Explain the difference between needs and wants.
4. Identify and describe the three sectors of industry.

Types of Business Organisations

Sole traders

A person who owns a business on their own is a **sole trader**. Sole traders are usually small businesses (ie with less than fifty employees) and do not usually operate on a national or international scale. Examples include local newsagents and hairdressers. The **objectives** of a sole trader may include: to survive, to make a profit and to provide a quality product.

Sole traders are usually **financed** through the owner's personal savings (this is known as capital), bank overdrafts or through loans from a bank or family/friends. Sole traders are sometimes able to get grants from the government or through other sources and these do not require to be paid back.

Advantages	Disadvantages
■ Easy to set up.	■ Owner has no one to share responsibility, workload or problems with.
■ Owner gets to keep profits.	
■ Owner can decide the hours to work.	■ Finance can be difficult to obtain.
■ Owner gets to make all the decisions which can be done quickly.	■ Unlimited liability for the owner.

Top Tip

You need to be able to describe different types of organisations with reference to who owns it, who controls it, its aims and how it is financed. You should also be able to suggest advantages and disadvantages of each type of business organisation.

Partnerships

A **partnership**, like a sole trader, is easy to set up and has between two to twenty partners. Each partner is an owner of the business. These types of businesses can be of different sizes and operate locally and nationally. Examples include doctors' surgeries, accountants and solicitors. You can sometimes tell by the name of the business whether it is a partnership. For example, the name 'Robinson & Biggs Accountants' would suggest that this business was a partnership. The **objectives** and **finance** available to partnerships are the same as sole traders, with the exception that extra capital can sometimes be available as there are more owners of the business who can bring this in.

Advantages	Disadvantages
■ Workload and responsibility shared.	■ Disagreements between partners could occur.
■ Each partner often brings different experiences and skills.	■ Each partner has unlimited liability.
	■ Profits are split between partners.
■ Easier to obtain finance than a sole trader.	■ A legal agreement between partners needs to be set up.
■ Shared risks and decision making.	

Limited companies

A **limited company** is different from a sole trader or partnership, because to be an owner you need to purchase shares and therefore become a **shareholder**. There are two types of limited companies: **Private Limited Companies** (Ltds) and **Public Limited Companies** (Plcs).

Private limited companies

Shares in a private limited company are not available for anyone to buy. Therefore, not everybody can be an owner of a private limited company. This type of company is owned by a minimum of one shareholder and is run by an appointed Board of Directors. By law, there must be at least one Director and a Company Secretary but shareholders are allowed to become Directors. When a private limited company is being set up, a Memorandum of Association and Articles of Association must be produced in accordance with the Companies Act.

The biggest advantage of setting up a private limited company, compared to a sole trader or partnership, is **limited liability**. This means if the company was to go bankrupt the owners of the company only lose the money they have invested. Their personal assets (eg home, car or any savings) are not at risk of being taken to pay for the failed company's debts. The opposite of limited liability is **unlimited liability**, which is what sole traders and partnerships have.

Objectives may include those for sole traders and partnerships but might also be to have a strong brand, to have high sales revenue and to grow.

Shares can be issued to raise **finance**. Finance can also be raised through bank loans, mortgages or government grants.

Advantages	Disadvantages
■ Limited liability for shareholders. ■ Responsibility and risk shared. ■ Experience and skills from shareholders and Directors. ■ More sources of finance available.	■ More complicated than a sole trader or partnership to set up. ■ Company to adhere to the rules and regulations of the Companies Act.

Public limited companies

The difference between this type of company and a private limited company is that shares are available to purchase by anyone via the stock market (hence the word 'public' in its title). There must be at least two shareholders who will own the company, but an appointed Board of Directors control and manage it. A Memorandum of Association and Articles of Association must also be produced.

Public limited companies tend to be large, with over 250 employees, and generally operate on an international scale. A Plc that is **multinational** will operate in more than one country and there are many advantages to this. There are lots of examples of this type of company, but well-known examples include Microsoft and Virgin.

The **objectives** of this company include: to become market leader, to improve social responsibility, to grow and to maximise profits.

The **finance** available is the same as for private limited companies, but shares can be sold more easily through the stock market.

Advantages	Disadvantages
■ Limited liability for shareholders. ■ More sources of finance available. ■ Because of their size, can take advantage of economies of scale.	■ Company to adhere to the rules and regulations of the Companies Act. ■ Annual company accounts are available publicly. ■ Shares can be purchased by anyone, therefore there is no control over ownership.

Top Tip

Do not confuse public limited companies with public sector organisations. These are completely different – make sure you know the differences!

Voluntary organisations

Voluntary organisations, as the name suggests, are managed and run by volunteers. These volunteers are willing to give up their time for no financial gain, usually because they have an interest in the organisation. Examples of voluntary organisations include the Scouts, Girl Guides and some youth and sports clubs. Voluntary organisations are mainly funded through donations and membership fees.

Charities

Charities exist for the purpose of helping a particular cause. This could be to raise money for children in poverty, to help suffering animals or to fund research for medical conditions. A register of all the charities that exist is kept by the government.

Charities receive much of their finance from donations (by the public or other organisations), government and lottery funding, through selling goods and from holding fundraising events. Children in Need, the Red Cross and the RSPB are examples of charities.

> **Top Tip**
>
> Charities and voluntary organisations do not exist to make a profit unlike sole traders, partnerships and limited companies.

Publicly funded organisations

Public sector organisations are managed by the government on behalf of the taxpayer who own them. They are mainly funded through taxes. The aims of these organisations are to provide services, to improve communities and societies and to act in the best interests of the general public.

There are different types of publicly funded organisations including **central government, local government** and **public sector corporations**.

Central government	Central government control and provide people with essential services such as Health, Defence and Transport. The Scottish Government (previously known as the Scottish Executive) is an example of central government. People are elected (voted in) to become members of central government and are known as politicians. Politicians control central government.
Local government	Local governments are responsible for providing services in a particular location. Glasgow City Council and Aberdeenshire Council are examples of local governments. Local governments have responsibility for schools, roads, council housing and leisure facilities in their area. They sometimes charge for using certain facilities (eg swimming pools and sporting facilities) and this, together with money from the taxpayer, fund local governments. Elected politicians control local governments and appointed managers run them.
Public corporations	Public corporations provide goods and services to the public and are owned by the government. They are sometimes referred to as **nationalised** industries. The BBC is an example of a public corporation. These organisations are funded by money from the government as well as money from the public for providing these services. A Chairperson and Board of Directors manage the organisation.

Franchises

A person who starts a business and provides a product or service supplied by another business is known as a **franchisee** and operates a business known as a **franchise**. The franchisee is allowed to use the **franchisor's** business name and sell its products.

There are advantages and disadvantages of franchising to the franchisor.

Advantages to the franchisor	Disadvantages to the franchisor
■ Franchisee provides a sum of money (which is usually a percentage of turnover) each year. ■ Risk is shared between the franchisee and franchisor.	■ The money received from the franchisee may be less than what the franchisor could have made if they had opened the business. ■ The franchisor's business name and image could be damaged as a result of a poor franchisee.

Advantages to the franchisee	Disadvantages to the franchisee
■ They are able to set up business using an already established name and brand. ■ Risk is shared between the franchisee and franchisor.	■ The franchisee may have little control over products and price. ■ Can be expensive to purchase and set up a franchise.

Burger King, McDonalds and Pizza Hut are examples of franchises. There has been a significant increase in the number of franchises over recent years.

Top Tip

There are many advantages of organisations operating in the public sector. Use your notes and the internet to help you make a list of these.

Sample examination questions

1. Compare the objectives of a public limited company with those of a charity. (6 marks)
2. Identify two sources of funding for a public sector organisation. (2 marks)
3. Explain three reasons why an organisation would become a private limited company. (3 marks)
4. Explain the advantages of franchising for a franchiser. (3 marks)

Quick Test 2

1. Identify the main aim of private sector organisations.
2. Identify the main aim of public sector and voluntary organisations.
3. Identify the main advantage of operating as a limited company compared to a sole trader or partnership.
4. Who owns public sector organisations and who manages them?
5. Describe what is meant by a multinational company.

Objectives

What are objectives?

Objectives are **targets or goals** that an organisation has; they provide the organisation and its workforce with something to work towards. Objectives show what the organisation would like to achieve over a period of time. They are important because they can be used to measure how successful an organisation is. An organisation will usually make its objectives public, for example in its mission statement and on its website.

Organisations will **make decisions** in order to find ways to meet their objectives. As an example, an organisation may make the decision to grow its overseas operations (ie to become multinational). To do this, they must find appropriate locations to expand to, recruit staff in these new locations and market their product to potential customers.

 Between objectives and different types of decisions that need to be made to achieve objectives.

Organisations and objectives

Different **types** of organisations will have different objectives. The main objective of a private sector business (eg sole trader or limited company) is profit maximisation or in other words, to make as much profit as possible. Whereas the main objective of a voluntary sector organisation (eg a charity) is not to maximise profit, but to provide a particular service.

Examples of private sector business objectives	Examples of voluntary sector business objectives
■ To survive. ■ To maximise profit. ■ To maximise sales. ■ To enlarge market share or to become the market leader. ■ To grow. ■ To provide a high quality product.	■ To provide a service. ■ To help those in need. ■ To raise as much money as possible. ■ To make the best use of money available. ■ To be socially responsible.

Some of the objectives **identified** above are **described** in more detail opposite. It is important to remember that the objectives of organisations may change over time and that some are more strategic (long term) than others.

Between different types of organisations and the objectives they may have.

Objectives in more detail

The table below shows you some objectives **identified** in the left-hand column with a **description** provided in the right-hand column. These objectives are **strategic**. This means they are long term and set the overall vision for the organisation.

Objective	Description
Profit maximisation	To make as much profit as possible by maximising sales and keeping the cost of sales low.
Sales maximisation	To generate as many sales as possible, therefore increasing revenue (the income/money from sales).
Survival	To survive/exist despite competitive or difficult economic conditions. This might mean having to make difficult decisions and cope with short-term cash flow problems.
Growth	To expand the organisation into new markets or into new countries. By growing, organisations can often take advantage of economies of sale (eg discounts for buying in large quantities) and minimise the risk of failure.
Become market leader	To control and dominate the market within which the organisation operates. This may involve eliminating (getting rid of) competition.
Social responsibility	To act and behave in a responsible and ethical way.
Provide a service	To support or help those in need through the provision of a service and to do this in the most efficient way possible.

Top Tip

Be **very** careful when answering questions on objectives. Make a note of whether the question asks for objectives of a particular type of organisation and whether it asks you to **identify** or **describe** these objectives. **At Higher level you will rarely be asked to only identify objectives.**

Sample examination questions

1. Describe two strategic objectives of a public sector organisation. (2 marks)
2. Identify two objectives of firms operating in a highly competitive market such as the mobile phone industry. (2 marks)
3. Why might growth be an objective for a firm? (4 marks)
4. Discuss the objectives of a Plc compared to a public sector organisation. (5 marks)

Quick Test 3

1. What are objectives?
2. Would an organisation in the voluntary or public sector aim to make a profit?
3. Describe the main objective of a private sector organisation.
4. If an objective was a strategic one, what would this mean?
5. At Higher level are you more likely to be asked to identify or describe objectives?

Stakeholders

What are stakeholders?

Stakeholders are interested in an organisation's success. A stakeholder could be a person, group (eg the local community) or another organisation (eg a bank or a supplier).

The two lists below show some of the different stakeholders for two different types of organisations: a public limited company and a charity. Make a note of which stakeholders are the same and which ones are different and then think about whether they are internal stakeholders (ie within the business) or external (ie outwith the business).

Stakeholders of a Public Limited Company

- Shareholders
- Local community
- Suppliers
- Board of Directors or management
- Customers
- Government (central and local)
- Employees
- Banks and other financial institutions

Stakeholders of a Charity

- Board of Trustees/volunteers
- Donors
- Bank
- Local community

Top Tip

Competitors are **not** stakeholders as they are not interested in the **success** of an organisation. A competitor would probably want the organisation to fail! Do not use competitors as an example of a stakeholder in a NAB or exam as it will gain no marks.

Interests and influence of stakeholders

Stakeholders each have different **interests** and **influences** in an organisation. The table below gives some examples.
Interest refers to why that stakeholder is concerned with the success of the organisation.
Influence refers to how much power that stakeholder has over the organisation and the actions that they can take which many benefit or disrupt the organisation's activities and/or objectives.

Stakeholder	Interest	Influence
Management	■ Want high profits and low costs. ■ Want large bonuses for their work.	■ Make decisions (eg what to produce, who to employ, what price to charge).
Employees	■ Want fair pay for their labour. ■ Want good working conditions. ■ Want to be treated fairly.	■ Can take industrial action, causing production to stop. ■ Can produce poor quality products. ■ Can leave employment.
Customers	■ Want high quality products. ■ Want to pay a low price. ■ Want to receive good customer service and high standards of after sales service.	■ Can buy products elsewhere if unhappy. ■ Can provide positive or negative feedback about the organisation.

Government	■ Want jobs to be provided. ■ Want money from taxation. ■ Want social and other economic benefits to be provided to communities.	■ Can introduce legislation for the organisation to follow. ■ Can change the amount of tax to be paid. ■ Can grant or refuse planning permission.
Local community	■ Want jobs in the local area. ■ Want to ensure the organisation does not damage or pollute the environment. ■ Want to receive social benefits (eg better roads and housing).	■ Can make complaints to the local council. ■ Can participate in protests. ■ Can provide positive or negative feedback about the organisation.
Suppliers	■ Want to receive payment for products provided. ■ Want repeat purchases.	■ Can change the amount to be paid for the products provided. ■ Can change the terms and conditions of service and delivery.

Top Tip

Make sure you understand the difference between a stakeholder's **interest** and **influence** in an organisation. Be able to give examples of why stakeholders are interested in an organisation and examples of what action stakeholders can take to influence it.

Sample examination questions

1. Describe how five different stakeholders could influence an organisation. (5 marks)
2. Describe how a local council may be influenced by its different stakeholders. (8 marks)

Quick Test 4

1. What is a stakeholder?
2. Identify four examples of a stakeholder.
3. Explain what is meant by stakeholder interest.
4. Explain what is meant by stakeholder influence.

Factors affecting Business Activity

Sources of financial assistance

We saw earlier in this chapter some of the different **sources of finance** available to different **types** of organisations. The availability of finance is a large factor impacting upon the operation of a business. A description of some of these sources of finance is given in the table below but this topic is dealt with in more detail in Chapter 8 – Finance.

Source	Description
Bank loan	A bank loan is a sum of money given to an organisation which must be paid back at a later date. Normally interest is charged on the loan.
Bank overdraft	An overdraft is when a bank agrees to an organisation taking more money out of their bank account than what is available. For example, if someone had £2000 in their bank account and wanted to take £3000 out of their account, their bank may give them a £1000 overdraft which would allow them to withdraw £3000 out of their account.
Mortgage	A mortgage is like a loan which is given to buy, eg the premises for an organisation, but the key difference is that the mortgage is **secured** against the property being bought.
Government grant	A grant is a sum of money given to an organisation that **does not** need to be paid back.

Top Tip

Think about each source and identify whether it is a long-term source or short-term source of finance. Also think about where it comes from – is it an internal source (from within the business) or external source (from outwith the business)?

The table above gives you a description of some sources of finance. However, there are many more! Some more examples that you should learn are given in the table below.

Source	Description
Share issues	Limited companies could issue extra shares. Plcs would issue these on the stock market.
Leasing	Leasing means to rent. Businesses could rent equipment, for example, rather than having to raise the finance to buy these outright.
Retained profits	Profits that are kept (hence the word 'retained' in its title) from previous years for later use.

Sources of finance are discussed in more detail in Chapter 8 – Finance. See page 90.

Between different types of organisations and the sources of finance suitable for them. Exam questions will often ask you for sources of finance for a particular **type of** organisation. Make sure you remember this when writing your answer!

Sources of assistance

Businesses sometimes need assistance or support to help them face the problems that today's business environment throws at them. Luckily, there are a number of places where businesses can go to for support.

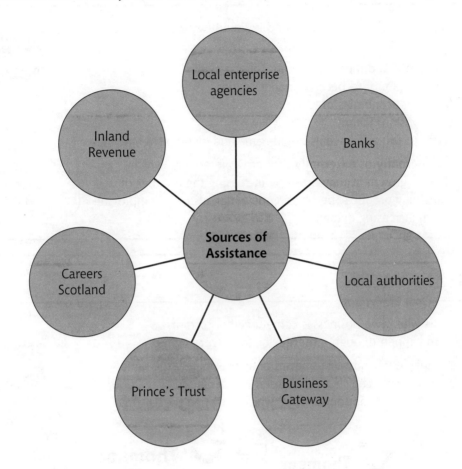

The organisations **identified** above can provide information and support on a variety of issues including advice on starting up, preparing business plans, advice on recording financial transactions, payroll and taxation. Some of these organisations may be able to give businesses financial support through a grant or loan.

Sample examination questions

1. Describe how organisations such as the Prince's Trust, banks and local enterprise agencies could provide assistance to a new business. (4 marks)

Sample examination questions for sources of finance are provided in Chapter 8 – Finance.

Quick Test 5

1. Identify three external sources of finance for a sole trader.
2. Describe a bank loan.
3. Identify three organisations where businesses can obtain support.
4. Identify three topics that a business could obtain assistance on.

Growth

Methods of growth

A strategic aim of a business may be to **grow** and it would want to do this for a number of reasons:

- To increase sales/profit and therefore returns for the owner(s)
- To increase market share or to become market leader
- To take advantage of economies of scale
- To reduce risk and risk of failure
- To become better known and have its brand name and identity strengthened

Businesses can grow **internally** or **externally**. If it grows internally, which is a very common method of growth, it may do so by increasing the number of stores it has, by selling new products, by entering new markets or by employing more staff to cope with increasing demand.

Top Tip

Make sure you understand the reasons why businesses grow as well as the different methods that can be used to grow a business.

External growth

External growth occurs when two businesses come together to form one business. This can happen through a **merger** or **takeover**.

Merger – a merger happens when two businesses of approximately the same size, agree to become one. First Choice and Thomson Fly merged in May 2009 to become the newly branded Thomson Airways, which is owned by TUI Travel.

First Choice ➕ Thomson ＝ Thomson Airways

Takeover – a takeover occurs when one larger business takes ownership and control of a smaller one. In 1999, the American company Wal-Mart took over ASDA. Both companies have retained their current brand identity.

WAL★MART   **ASDA**

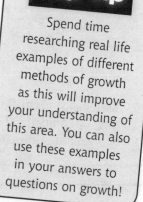

Top Tip

Spend time researching real life examples of different methods of growth as this will improve your understanding of this area. You can also use these examples in your answers to questions on growth!

Integration

When two businesses providing the same service or selling the same product join together this is known as **horizontal integration**; the merger of First Choice and Thomson Fly is a good example. They have now eliminated competition from one another, as well as increasing market share. The merged company will be able to take greater advantage of economies of scale and reduce its operating costs in a number of areas.

When businesses in a similar industry, but who operate at different stages of production, join together, this is known as **vertical integration**. This can be divided further into <u>backward</u> vertical integration and <u>forward</u> vertical integration. Vertical integration allows businesses to have more control over the production or distribution process by cutting out the 'middle-man'.

➡️

Fisherman   **Fish Market**   **Fish and Chip Shop**

Backward Vertical Integration
(taking over a supplier)

Forward Vertical Integration
(taking over a customer)

When two businesses that provide completely different services or sell different goods from each other join together, this is called **conglomerate integration** and they are said to have diversified. **Diversification** has many benefits including risk reduction; if one fails, for example because of decreasing demand for that product or service, then it would be very unlucky if the other one also failed!

De-merger and divestment

De-mergers occur when one business splits into two separate organisations and **divestment** is when a business sells some of its assets or part of its company to another. They may do either of these two things if they are not making enough profit from that particular activity or to raise extra finance. They can then use this finance to expand on their core operations or for investment in other activities.

Sample examination questions

1. Describe how both horizontal and vertical integration could allow an organisation to become even larger and more profitable. (5 marks)
2. Discuss the ways in which divestment and de-merger can assist the growth of an organisation. (4 marks)
3. Moving into new markets such as China is an example of growth. Describe other methods of growth. (6 marks)

Quick Test 6

1. Identify three reasons why a business would want to grow.
2. Explain the difference between a merger and a takeover.
3. Describe the difference between backward vertical integration and forward vertical integration.
4. Describe the term de-merger.

Business as a Dynamic Activity

Internal and external influences on organisations

All organisations face a number of things that impact upon what they do and the way they do it. We can group these things into two groups: **internal factors** and **external factors**. Internal factors are things within the organisation that impact upon the way it operates and external factors are things outwith the organisation's control that impact upon the way it operates. All organisations must respond to these factors by changing the way it operates or it runs the risk of failing.

Internal Factors

- Availability of finance
- New product developments
- Changes in costs
- Quality and skills of employees and management
- Company policy
- Availability of appropriate ICT
- Corporate culture

Top Tip

Think about the impact and possible consequences of each internal and external factor on business. Make a list of these.

External factors

The external factors impacting upon business can be remembered by simply remembering what **PESTEC** stands for! The table below shows you examples of external factors under the PESTEC heading, which all impact upon the way businesses operate. Throughout this book you will see references to external factors and you should refer to this page when you do so.

P – Political	E – Economic
■ UK, EU and international law	■ Interest rates
■ Government policies at local and national levels	■ Exchange rates
■ Provision of essential infrastructure such as roads and schools	■ Levels of inflation
■ Rates of taxation	■ Levels of unemployment
■ Provision of funding under certain circumstances (eg locating to a particular area)	■ The business cycle (periods of 'booms' and 'slumps' in the economy) reflecting changes in consumer demand
S – Social	**T – Technological**
■ Changes in culture, trends and fashion	■ Technology is advancing quickly and methods of communication are constantly changing
■ Changes in demographics (the number of people who live in particular locations)	■ Use of technology in production is constantly changing and advancing
■ Increase in work/life balance demanded by employees	■ Greater emphasis on businesses becoming paperless
■ Changing working practices and family-friendly arrangements	■ Growth of e-commerce

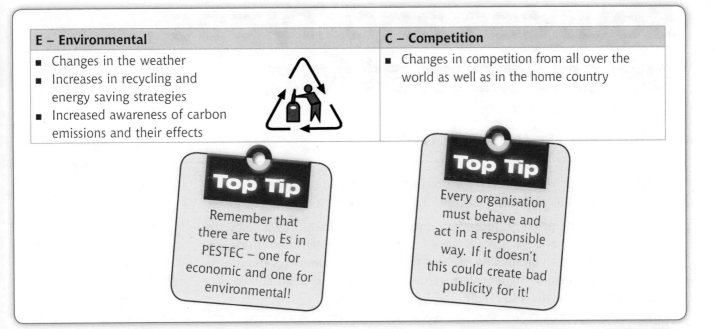

E – Environmental	C – Competition
■ Changes in the weather ■ Increases in recycling and energy saving strategies ■ Increased awareness of carbon emissions and their effects	■ Changes in competition from all over the world as well as in the home country

Top Tip

Remember that there are two Es in PESTEC – one for economic and one for environmental!

Top Tip

Every organisation must behave and act in a responsible way. If it doesn't this could create bad publicity for it!

The changing business environment

There are other factors which have impacted upon and continue to influence the way organisations operate today. For example, there has been an increase in the significance of multinational companies, and the important contribution smaller organisations make to the economy has been recognised. Continual advancement in technology and the increase in competitiveness of other organisations continue to be major influences in the activities of organisations.

Sample examination questions

1. Explain how external factors may affect an organisation. (6 marks)
2. Identify and explain three economic factors that can affect the profitability of an organisation. (6 marks)
3. Legislation is one example of a political external influence. Describe three other examples of external influence on an organisation. (3 marks)

Entrepreneur	Sole trader	Objectives	Public corporation
External influences	Stakeholders	Partnership	Creating wealth
Public limited company	Franchise	Consumption	De-merger
Private limited company	Production	Integration	Growth
Sectors of industry	Merger	Takeover	Divestment
Factors of production	Charities	Public sector	Franchise
Unlimited liability	Voluntary organisations	Adding value	Limited liability

Quick Test 7

1. Why must businesses respond to changes in the business environment?
2. Identify what the letters PESTEC stand for.
3. Identify two political factors that impact upon business.
4. Identify two economic factors that impact upon business.
5. Has there been an increase or decrease in the importance of the contribution of small organisations to the economy?

Sources and Types of Information

Sources of information

Information is data which has been processed and presented in a meaningful way. There are many different **types** of information that come from a number of **sources**.

Information can be **primary, secondary, internal** or **external**. Shown below are a description and some examples of these four sources of information. To be able to assess the **value** and **reliability** of these sources of information (as this is an essential requirement at Higher level), we must consider the benefits and costs of each source so these are also given.

Top Tip

Remember that **sources** and **types** of information are different. Be careful not to confuse these!

Primary	Description	Examples
	Primary information is new information that has been gathered by an organisation and will be used for a specific purpose.	Information gathered from a survey/ questionnaire, interview or observation.
	Benefits – primary information is of value to an organisation because they know where it has come from as they have collected it themselves; it should therefore be correct. It will be up-to-date. *Costs – it is costly as well as time-consuming to collect.*	

Secondary	Description	Examples
	Secondary information has been used for another purpose and is therefore 'old'.	Information on internet websites, textbooks, newspapers, magazines, on CD Roms, or government statistics.
	Benefits – it is cheaper and easier to obtain than primary information. *Costs – as it has been used for another purpose, it may not be complete nor free from bias. It could be out-of-date.*	

Internal	Description	Examples
	Information gathered within the organisation from its own records.	Staff records and final accounts.
	Benefits – usually more fit for purpose and relevant to the decision being made or task in hand. As the source is known it is more likely to be reliable. It can usually be accessed easily and quickly. *Costs – only useful if the information (eg staff records) has been kept up-to-date. It may be costly to set up and maintain systems to store internal information.*	

External	Description	Examples
	Information gathered from sources outwith the organisation.	Information from market research, newspapers, competitors' websites and government reports.
	Benefits – often easy and cost effective to obtain. *Costs – often unreliable as the source is unknown and cannot be checked. It may not be complete and might not be free from bias.*	

Types of information

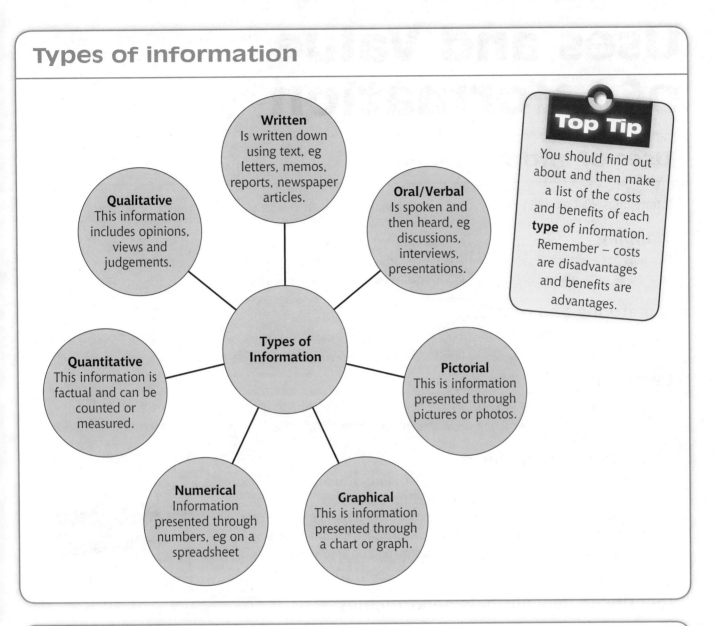

Written
Is written down using text, eg letters, memos, reports, newspaper articles.

Oral/Verbal
Is spoken and then heard, eg discussions, interviews, presentations.

Qualitative
This information includes opinions, views and judgements.

Quantitative
This information is factual and can be counted or measured.

Types of Information

Pictorial
This is information presented through pictures or photos.

Numerical
Information presented through numbers, eg on a spreadsheet

Graphical
This is information presented through a chart or graph.

Top Tip

You should find out about and then make a list of the costs and benefits of each **type** of information. Remember – costs are disadvantages and benefits are advantages.

Sample examination questions

1. Describe two suitable types of information required by someone selecting a holiday. Justify your choices. (4 marks)
2. Distinguish between the terms quantitative and qualitative information. (2 marks)

Quick Test 8

1. Identify two examples of primary information.
2. Identify two examples of secondary information.
3. Describe a reason why primary information may be of higher quality than secondary information.
4. Explain the difference between internal and external information.
5. Explain the difference between qualitative and quantitative information.
6. Identify two examples of written information.
7. Identify two examples of oral information.

Uses and Value of Information

Uses of information

Information is all around us and is used every day in business. It can be used for a variety of purposes.

Planning

Planning means thinking ahead and about the future. It will involve using information to help inform new plans or in making predictions about what may happen in the future.

Monitoring and control

This involves using information to check how well the organisation is doing. Once this has been done, it may involve making decisions on how to improve the organisation's performance.

Decision making

High quality information is essential as this helps to make sure that the right decision is made. If poor information is used and the wrong decision is made, there could be serious consequences to the organisation.

Measuring performance

Information is used to check an organisation's financial performance. For example, information on actual sales performance can be used to measure whether the organisation is meeting its sales targets. This information can be used to make a comparison against previous years' performance or against the performance of competitors by carrying out ratio analysis (see page 86). Information on an organisation's performance will be used in future planning and decision making.

Top Tip

You should be able to describe the uses of information in business and be able to explain why information is important for these uses.

Identifying new business opportunities

Organisations can use information to see where there are opportunities to meet the needs and wants of more customers by coming up with a new business idea and then developing it. Information gathered from market research (see page 60) will be particularly useful.

Value of information

Information that organisations use needs to be of a very **high quality** because this means it has value for the organisation. If it is not, it could mean that decisions are made based on the wrong information and this could have serious consequences for the organisation.

We can assess the value of information by asking certain questions about the particular piece of information. More 'yes' answers will mean that the piece of information is of a higher quality and higher value than those pieces of information for which the answer was 'no'. Information which is assessed as being of a poor quality should be disregarded and not used in decision making.

Top Tip

The characteristics or features associated with high quality information have been **emboldened** in the question column of this table.

Question	What does this mean?
Is it **accurate**?	This means asking if the piece of information is correct and does not have any errors in it.
Is it **timely**?	This means asking if the piece of information is available when it is needed and is the most up-to-date available.
Is it **complete**?	This means asking if the piece of information has all of the required facts and nothing has been left out.
Is it **appropriate**?	This means asking if the piece of information is actually required for the purpose it will be used for.
Is it **available**?	This means asking if the piece of information will be accessible and available when needed.
Is it **cost effective**?	This means asking if the piece of information will be worth the cost to obtain it.
Is it **objective**?	This means asking if the piece of information will be free from bias.
Is it **concise**?	This means asking if the piece of information is brief (ie doesn't contain irrelevant material) and to the point.

Top Tip

Try to remember at least some of the features associated with good quality information. You must also be able to describe what these features mean.

Sample examination questions

1. High quality and reliable information is essential if a manager is to make effective decisions. Describe the characteristics of high quality, reliable information. (4 marks)
2. Discuss the reliability and value of the information that is available to consumers choosing a holiday. (8 marks)

Quick Test 9

1. Identify three uses of information in business.
2. Explain what is meant by using information to measure performance.
3. Suggest a reason why information must be of value to a business.
4. Identify five characteristics associated with high quality information.
5. Explain what is meant by information being accurate.

Business and ICT

Uses of ICT in business

ICT stands for **Information and Communications Technology** and is more than 'just computers'! A range of ICT is used in business today for a number of different reasons:

- To assist in decision making
- To collect and distribute information
- To communicate with different people
- To maintain a variety of records
- To assist in the product design and manufacturing process

Different pieces of **hardware** and **software** can be used to carry out the tasks given above.

What's the difference between hardware and software?

Hardware describes items which can be seen and touched, such as a computer monitor or printer. Software describes instructions in a computer language which tells the computer how to work. These sometimes come on a disk which needs to be installed before it will work.

Top Tip

Past exam questions have asked how ICT can be used to market products, to communicate with others and in the decision making process. You could refer to types of ICT as well as types of software in your answer to these questions.

Types of ICT

Different types of ICT are used in business. These include e-mail, networks, videoconferencing, internet websites and Computer Aided Manufacture (CAM).

Type of ICT	What is it and when is it used?
E-mail	E-mail is when you send an electronic message to another person via their e-mail address from your electronic mailbox. It is can be used to communicate with customers, other staff or suppliers who may be located all over the world.
Networks	A network is a group of computers linked together. These computers could be in different locations. They are used by organisations to share information.
Videoconferencing	Videoconferencing is when a computer link is set up between people in different locations. Different pieces of equipment such as a monitor, microphone and speaker system are used to see and hear the people who are participating in the videoconference. It is often used to hold meetings between groups of people who are in different locations.
Internet website	An internet website is a collection of information in one place which can be seen by typing in a website address (a URL) into a program such as *Internet Explorer*. An organisation may have a website to communicate information about its products and also to sell products online; this is known as e-commerce. Organisations can target customers worldwide through a website and if they use e-commerce to sell to customers they are able to sell online 24/7. Customers may also be able to take advantage of online discounts, access up-to-date product information and compare the products with others. *More information on internet selling and internet websites is provided on page 55.*
Computer Aided Manufacture (CAM)	This involves using computer-controlled equipment and robots in the manufacturing of a product. Products can be produced of a more consistent quality than by hand.

Types of software

What is it and when is it used?

Word processing

Word processing software allows text to be entered, edited and presented in a suitable format. It could be used to create letters, reports, memos, posters or newsletters.

Database

Database software allows a collection of related information to be stored, retrieved and edited quickly. It is used to store information about customers, employees or suppliers. Database software can hold a huge quantity of information which can be easily sorted, searched and presented in a number of different ways depending on the user's specific requirements.

Top Tip

Different types of ICT and software are used to carry out different types of tasks. Some are more suitable for different tasks than others.

Spreadsheet

Spreadsheet software allows numerical information to be stored, retrieved and edited quickly. It can be used to store financial information (eg sales figures) or stock levels. Spreadsheet software uses lots of different formulae typed in by the user which tells the software what information the user would like. It has improved decision making by allowing 'what-if' scenarios to be created. What-if scenarios can be used to see what the impact would be on the business, eg if demand for a product fell. Graphs and charts can also be produced which can be useful in presenting complex numerical information.

Presentation software

Presentation software allows presentations to be created and shown electronically usually through a projector onto a screen. Presentation software can make presentations look much more professional by for example, adding in hyperlinks, animations and sound. This can make a presentation much more interesting!

Computer Aided Design (CAD)

This software allows products to be designed in 3D on a computer. Changes can easily be made and will show what a finished product would look like. It is much quicker using CAD rather than having to draw designs on paper!

Sample examination questions

1. ICT is used to help head office communicate effectively with branches in remote areas of the country. Explain how modern technology can be used to communicate effectively within an organisation. (6 marks)
2. Outline the factors that might restrict the use of technology. (4 marks)
3. Explain how ICT (Information Communications Technology) could support an organisation in the areas of marketing, human resources and finance. (5 marks)

Quick Test 10

1. Identify three reasons why businesses use ICT.
2. Suggest a reason why videoconferencing is useful when holding a meeting.
3. Identify what the letters CAM stand for.
4. Identify the piece of software that would be used to store customers' names and addresses.
5. Suggest a reason why spreadsheets are useful in decision making.

Benefits and Costs of ICT

Benefits of ICT

Using ICT and modern technology in business can have many advantages for an organisation, for example:

- Increased work rate and productivity.
- Data and information can be processed much more quickly than manually.
- Improved decision making as more information (and often better quality information) can be accessed.
- Lower employee wage costs if technology replaces the need for them.
- Communication between departments, branches and customers can improve.
- Wastage reduced as fewer errors are made.
- Production quality is more consistent.

Top Tip

Remember – benefits are advantages and costs are disadvantages. Costs can be more than just financial.

Costs of ICT

- Can be expensive to install and maintain hardware/software.
- Employees require training in using technology.
- Employees may be reluctant to use new technologies and may be resistant to change.
- Employees may feel unvalued and less motivated if they feel technology is replacing their jobs or parts of their jobs.
- Technology can break down and have faults; this is costly not only in terms of getting it fixed, but also time and, if production stops, the organisation's output.
- Legislation (see below) can restrict what information organisations can collect and store.
- Introducing procedures and policies to comply with legislation could be time consuming and costly.

Top Tip

ICT not only has an impact on an organisation, but also its employees. This impact can be positive (eg increased productivity) as well as negative (eg financial cost).

ICT and the law

The government has introduced laws that govern the way organisations use information and the way computers can be used. These laws help to protect individuals and organisations. Organisations that do not comply with the law will face prosecution and often severe penalties.

Data Protection Act 1998

The Data Protection Act governs the way organisations collect, store, process and distribute information. The Act has eight main principles:

- Data should be obtained and processed fairly.
- Data held should be adequate, relevant and not excessive for the purpose.
- Data should not be held longer than is necessary.
- Data can only be held for specific and lawful purposes.
- Data should be accurate and up-to-date.
- Individuals are entitled access to the data held about them.

- If appropriate the data should be altered to ensure it is accurate or deleted if no longer necessary.
- Security of the data should be maintained to ensure no unlawful access to the data can take place.

If a person thinks that an organisation is holding information about them which is wrong or misleading, they are able to complain to the **Data Protection Registrar**. The organisation can then be told to correct it.

Computer Misuse Act 1990

The Computer Misuse Act is concerned with those people who intend to or have committed the offence of hacking into computer systems. The Act makes it illegal for people to:
- gain access to computer material without permission
- gain unauthorised access with intent to commit or facilitate commission of further offences
- modify computer material without permission.

Top Tip

Questions on ICT and the law have been very popular in the examination paper over the past few years. You should consider not just the principles of each piece of legislation, but the impact it has on an organisation.

Freedom of Information Act 2000

The Freedom of Information Act has made it possible for people to request, from a public body, information that is held about them. People must be told if the public body holds information about them and they have the right to see it within 20 days. Some information may, however, under the Act, be withheld from the person requesting to see it if is concerned with, eg national security.

Sample examination questions

1. The use of most up-to-date technology is extremely important in the music industry. Describe the benefits to an organisation of investing in new technology. (5 marks)
2. Describe the legislation which protects consumers from misuse of information held about them. (6 marks)
3. The Data Protection Act 1998 is the legislation which covers information stored on computers about individuals. Describe the main features of the Data Protection Act. (5 marks)

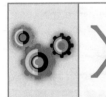

Internet website	CAD	Quantitative	Value
CAM	Secondary	Primary	Oral
Written	Data Protection	Freedom of Information	Software
Computer Misuse	Numerical	Pictorial	Graphical
Internal	Video conferencing	Networks	External

Quick Test 11

1. Will introducing technology help to increase or decrease an organisation's wages bill? Explain your answer.
2. Suggest a reason why modern technologies can help to make improved decisions.
3. Suggest a reason why employees can sometimes become less motivated when technology is introduced.
4. Identify the piece of legislation concerned with allowing people to request information held about them from a public body.
5. Identify the piece of legislation that states 'data should be accurate and up-to-date'.

Management and Decision Making

Managers and decision making

Organisations must make decisions to achieve objectives and to improve their performance. These decisions are made by managers who have the authority to make them. Decision making involves choosing the best option from a range of options. Managers have various functions to carry out when making decisions.

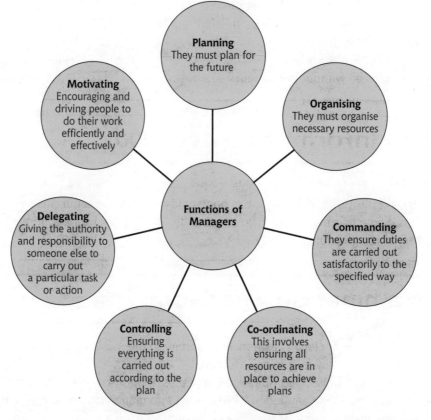

People who are in a management position have a very important role to perform in the organisation and will have been selected based on the skills and qualities that they have. Managers must be able to work well with other people, review and assess different situations and, where necessary, make decisions to ensure the organisation meets its objectives.

Types of decisions

Managers are involved in making different types of decisions.

Strategic

What are they?

They are long-term decisions that are concerned with the overall direction and focus of the organisation.

Who makes them?

Strategic decisions are made by the senior management of an organisation.

Examples
- To expand into a foreign country.
- To diversify into new products.
- To merge with another company.

Tactical

What are they?

They are medium-term decisions that are concerned with actions to achieve strategic decisions.

Who makes them?

Tactical decisions are made by the senior and middle management of an organisation.

Operational

What are they?

They are short-term decisions that affect the day-to-day running of the organisation.

Who makes them?

Operational decisions are usually made by low level managers (eg supervisor, department manager, team leader) but employees may also be involved in making them.

Examples

- Find cheaper suppliers of raw materials in order to cut costs.
- Expand range of goods or services offered.
- Seek opportunities to sell goods or services in locations where they don't already.
- Develop a new marketing campaign to raise awareness of the organisation's products.

Examples

- Training staff in new products available.
- Decisions on staff working hours for next week.

The decisions that managers make will help an organisation achieve certain objectives. For example, deciding to expand the goods or services offered is a tactical decision and would help to achieve the strategic objective of growth and profit maximisation. It may also contribute to achieving an increase in market share.

> Between making different types of decisions and achieving objectives.

The right decision?

Managers must **evaluate** all decisions they have made to establish whether or not they have made the correct one. They will look at and consider various pieces of evidence and information when doing this. For example, they will look at sales and profit figures, how staff reacted to the decision (has there been a decrease in attendance at work?) and, where appropriate, how customers have responded.

Sample examination questions

1. Describe three tactical decisions that could lead to growth. (3 marks)
2. Describe, using examples, the three types of decisions taken by organisations in order to achieve their objectives. (6 marks)
3. Describe how a manager could assess the effectiveness of a decision. (4 marks)

Quick Test 12

1. What is decision making?
2. Identify the five functions of managers in decision making.
3. Explain the difference between a strategic decision and a tactical decision.
4. Identify two examples of a tactical decision.

Decision Making Models

Structured decision making

Managers go through a series of stages when engaged in decision making. These stages can be best remembered by remembering the acronym **POGADSCIE**.

	Stage	What does this mean?
P	Identify the **P**roblem	This means identifying the problem or issue that needs to be resolved.
O	Identify the **O**bjectives	This means considering the objective(s) that need to be achieved when making the decision.
G	**G**ather information	This means gathering information from a variety of sources (primary and secondary) to aid the decision making process.
A	**A**nalyse the gathered information	This means looking very carefully and questioning the information that has been gathered. It is also concerned with assessing the quality of the information gathered.
D	**D**evise possible solutions	This means making a list of solutions to the problem in question.
S	**S**elect the best solution	This means choosing the best solution from the range of possible solutions to solve the problem as effectively as possible. There may be internal and external factors that impact upon the solution chosen.
C	**C**ommunicate the decision	This means informing people (eg staff) of the decision that has been made.
I	**I**mplement the decision	This means taking action to put into practice the solution that has been chosen.
E	**E**valuate the effectiveness of the decision and the influence of ICT	This means considering how successful the decision has been (has it solved or helped the problem?) and how ICT has influenced the success of the decision. Changes may need to be made to the solution to ensure it continues to solve the problem and improves future performance.

There are benefits of using structured decision making models (eg POGADSCIE) for an organisation:

- No quick decisions are made because time is given to gather information.
- Time is given to think about and consider the range of options (alternatives) available.
- Factors (internal and external) that may impact upon the decision can be considered provided time permits.
- The effectiveness and impact of each decision is considered during the evaluation stage.

However, there are also costs:

- It takes time to gather information and it may be difficult to obtain good quality information (and expensive!).
- The impact of each solution cannot be fully seen.
- It may be difficult to think of different solutions.
- Instinct and gut reactions to situations are stifled.

Top Tip

Spend time learning the **POGADSCIE** model and the benefits and costs of using a structured decision making model.

SWOT analysis

Organisations can carry out a **SWOT analysis** which is a method of identifying the internal and external factors which influence an organisation and therefore what will impact upon the organisation's decision making process.

Strengths and weaknesses are concerned with the organisation and its current position; opportunities and threats are concerned with the external environment and the impact it may have on the future of the organisation. An organisation wants to build on its strengths, improve its weaknesses, take advantage of opportunities and minimise the impact of threats.

STRENGTHS	WEAKNESSES
What is the organisation doing well?	What is the organisation doing not so well?
OPPORTUNITIES	**THREATS**
Where are there opportunities for the organisation to improve its performance and profitability?	What factors are outwith the organisation's control that may impact upon its activities?

Top Tip

Try carrying out your own SWOT analysis on a company. You could also carry out a SWOT analysis on yourself to see what your strengths, weaknesses, opportunities and threats are in relation to this course!

Sample examination questions

1. Describe the benefits of using a decision making model in order to solve problems. (6 marks)
2. Organisations may choose to assess their strengths, weaknesses, opportunities and threats before making important decisions. Describe the costs and benefits of using a SWOT analysis in decision making. (5 marks)

Quick Test 13

1. Identify the nine stages of a structured decision making model.
2. Suggest two benefits of using a structured decision making model.
3. Suggest two costs of using a structured decision making model.
4. What does SWOT stand for?

What Makes Decision Making Difficult?

Internal factors

There are factors within the organisation that can impact upon what decision is made and also the quality of that decision. The internal constraints of an organisation on its decision making process may have been identified when analysing its strengths and weaknesses during a SWOT analysis.

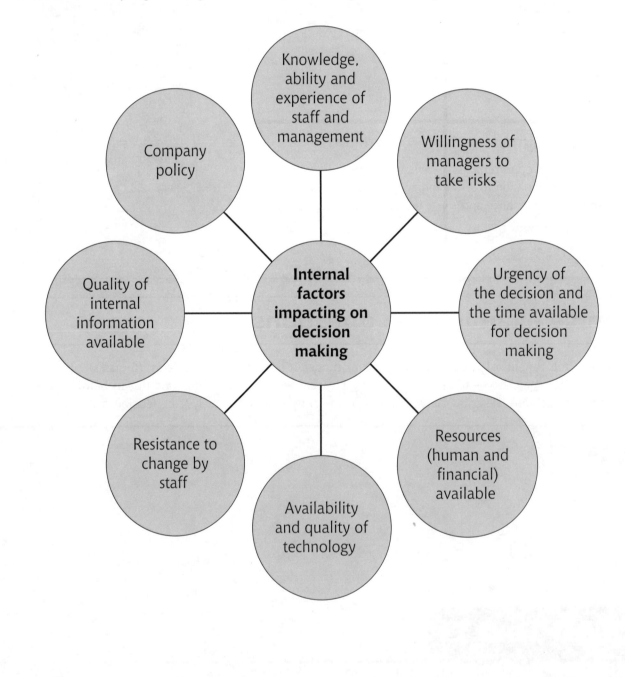

External factors

There are factors outwith an organisation's control that will impact upon the decision being made and also the quality of the decision. The external factors that need to be considered when an organisation is making a decision may have been identified when analysing opportunities and threats during a SWOT analysis. The significance of each factor will be dependant on the decision being made and the possible impact and consequences of that factor on the decision.

See page 22 for more information on external factors.

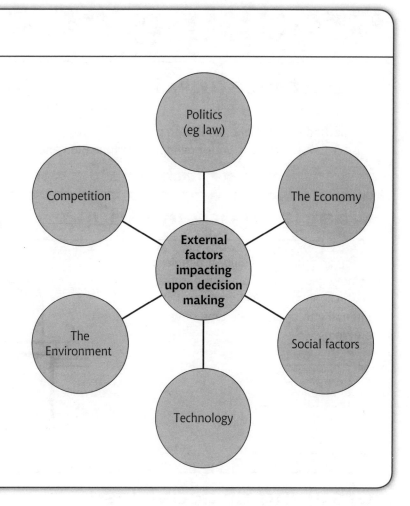

Between decision making and PESTEC.

Sample examination questions

1. Explain the factors that could affect the quality of a decision made by a manager. (4 marks)
2. Describe internal constraints that can make decision making difficult. (6 marks)
3. Discuss the factors that might affect the **quality** of a decision. (5 marks)

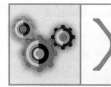

Decision making model	SWOT analysis	Internal factors
Strategic	Tactical	Operational
External factors	POGADSCIE	Objectives
PESTEC		

Quick Test 14

1. Identify three internal factors that impact upon the decision making process.
2. Identify two resources required when implementing a decision.
3. Explain what is meant by external factors.

Grouping of Activities

Important study note

This section on internal organisation will not be assessed in any internal assessment (NAB). However, it is subject to assessment in your preliminary examination and in the final SQA examination. Be prepared!

What is an organisation?

An organisation is a group of people who come together for a common purpose, aim or goal. Organisations will organise themselves internally to best suit the type of work they are doing.

Grouping of activities

Top Tip

Grouping of activities has been a popular topic in the final examination in recent years. Make sure you study previous exam papers carefully to see examples of the types of questions that are asked.

Organisations can group their activities in a number of ways, depending on a number of factors:

- Size of the organisation
- Technology used and availability
- The market the organisation targets
- The product (good or service) being sold

Grouping	Description
Functional	Functional grouping means grouping by department. People working in these departments will have similar tasks to carry out. The departments that exist will likely be Human Resources, Operations, Marketing, Finance and Research & Development.

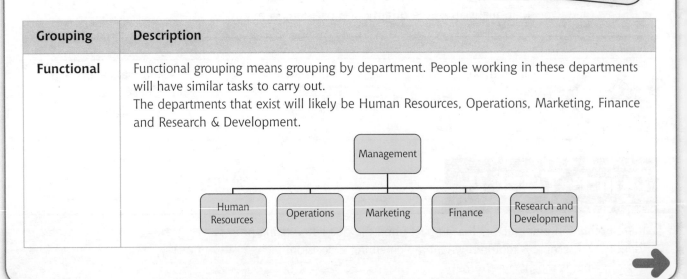

Product/ service	Product/service grouping means grouping each department based on a different product that the organisation sells. Each department will concentrate on their product which will result in an increase in specialist knowledge of that product.

Top Tip

Make a list of each type of activity grouping with a description of it and then do some research to find out the advantages and disadvantages of each type of activity grouping.

The Virgin Group have their activities grouped by product/service. This enables each department to concentrate on their own product/service.

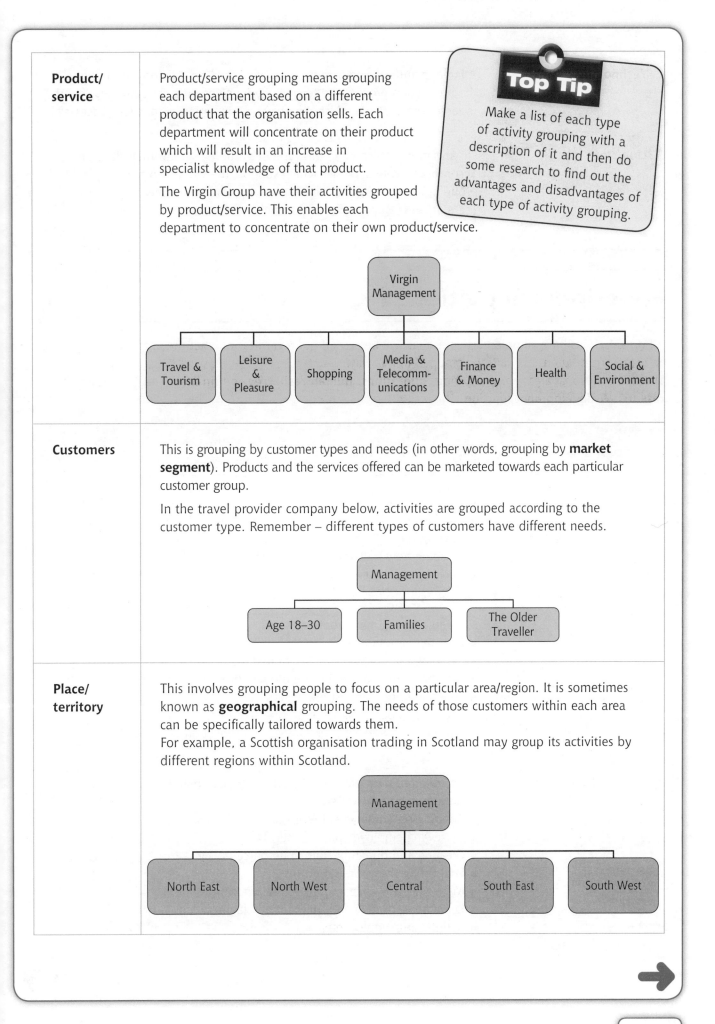

This is grouping by customer types and needs (in other words, grouping by **market segment**). Products and the services offered can be marketed towards each particular customer group.

In the travel provider company below, activities are grouped according to the customer type. Remember – different types of customers have different needs.

Customers

Place/ territory

This involves grouping people to focus on a particular area/region. It is sometimes known as **geographical** grouping. The needs of those customers within each area can be specifically tailored towards them.

For example, a Scottish organisation trading in Scotland may group its activities by different regions within Scotland.

Technology	A large manufacturing organisation may group its activities according to the production process and technology involved. This is commonly found in large organisations which may have many varied production processes.
Line/staff	Organisations which have this type of grouping, group their departments according to core activities which support the work of other people (staff grouping) and line grouping being groups of management (eg managers, supervisors and so on).

Functional activities

All organisations have common activities that will be carried out regardless of what the organisation's product is. Some organisations may also be grouped in this way.

The four functional areas are **marketing, operations, human resources** and **finance.** There may also be a **research & development** function.

Function	Examples of activities
Marketing	■ Deciding what to produce and sell. ■ Conducting market research. ■ Advertising and promoting products. ■ Deciding how much to charge for each product. ■ Deciding the best way to get the product to the customer.
Operations	■ Manufacturing new products. ■ Distributing products. ■ Deciding upon which supplier of raw materials to use. ■ Employing methods to ensure product quality. ■ Deciding upon the best production method. ■ Managing stock using an appropriate system. ■ Carrying out work studies to measure production efficiency.
Human Resources	■ Recruitment and selection of staff across the organisation. ■ Arranging training for staff. ■ Advising on employment terms and conditions. ■ Reviewing employee pay structures. ■ Creating and updating Human Resource policies. ■ Supporting the appraisal process. ■ Managing grievance and discipline procedures. ■ Keeping up-to-date with relevant emplayment legislation. ■ Maintaining employee records.

Finance	<ul><li>Receiving and processing requests for payments (ie bills).</li><li>Arranging for the payment of employee wages.</li><li>Preparing budgets.</li><li>Preparing final accounts.</li><li>Carrying out financial analysis using ratios.</li><li>Preparing financial information for management decision making.</li><li>Presenting the financial position to management and other stackholders.</li></ul>

These topics are dealt with in more detail in Chapters 6–9.

Quick Test 15

1. Identify the four main functional areas.
2. Describe the main feature of an organisation grouped by product/service.
3. Describe the main feature of an organisation grouped by customer.
4. Identify two activities carried out by the Human Resources department.
5. Identify two activities carried out by the Finance department.

Organisation Structures

What are they?

An **organisation structure** shows how an organisation is structured and will often be presented as an **organisation chart.**

An organisation chart shows.

- Who has overall responsibility for the organisation
- The levels of authority and responsibility within the organisation
- The lines of communication and chain of command
- The span of control within the organisation
- Different relationships between people within the organisation.

Top Tip

Draw an organisation chart wherever you can on questions to do with grouping of activities and organisation structures.

Organisation structures: key terms

You may come across many terms when learning about organisations and how they are structured. Some of the most common terms are:

Term	Definition
Span of control	The number of **subordinates** (people) who report to a person. A wide span of control will mean that many people report to one person and a narrow span of control will mean that very few people report to one person. 
Chain of command	This shows how instructions are passed down through an organisation. A long chain of command may mean communication and decision making takes longer compared to a short chain of command.
Authority	This means having the power to make decisions and to take particular actions.
Responsibility	This means being answerable for decisions and actions taken.
Delegation	This means giving the authority and responsibility to someone else to carry out a particular task or action.

Types of organisation structures

Hierarchical	These are traditional structures with many layers of management and therefore a long chain of command. They are sometimes referred to as 'tall' structures. Instructions and decisions are passed down while information flows down and up. These structures tend to be found in organisations such as the army or the police force.

Flat	Flat structures contain few layers of management and therefore a short chain of command. Communication can occur more quickly compared to a hierarchical structure and information can flow around more easily and quickly. This type of structure tends to be found in smaller organisations, for example a dentist's surgery.
Matrix	Matrix (or task-based) structures tend to be formed for a specific reason, for example to work on a particular project or task. People will come together from various departments within the organisation to form the matrix structure. When the task or project has been completed, the matrix structure will become obsolete. A Project or Team Leader will be appointed to take charge of the task or project in hand. This structure can be motivating to staff and useful for solving complex problems.
Entrepreneurial	These are commonly found in smaller organisations, when decisions are made by the owner or manager with very little input from other people – which in turn demotivates employees. However, entrepreneurial structures allow for quicker decision making. It is not a common structure in larger organisations because management would carry too much of a heavy workload. Make sure you do not get mixed up with the **role of the entrepreneur** and an **entrepreneurial organisation structure**.
Centralised	This is when decisions are made by the senior management of a company, with little involvement from staff further down the chain of command. This type of structure is associated with a hierarchical structure and decisions are made by those who are skilled at doing so. It allows for a standardised approach across the organisation and avoids any conflicting approaches throughout the organisation.
Decentralised	This is the opposite of a centralised organisation structure, whereby the authority (the power) to make decisions has been delegated to departments and subordinates further down the chain of command. This type of structure is associated with a flat structure and the advantages that it brings. Staff become **empowered** and this in turn will motivate them – provided they want the extra responsibility in the first place!

Sample examination questions

1. Organisations often use an entrepreneurial structure. Explain the advantages and disadvantages of an entrepreneurial structure. (4 marks)
2. Many organisations group their activities by function. Discuss other methods an organisation could use to group their activities. (8 marks)
3. Local managers are 'empowered' to make decisions. Describe the advantages and disadvantages of decentralised decision making. (6 marks)

Quick Test 16

1. What is an organisation chart?
2. Explain the difference between a narrow and a wide span of control.
3. Explain what is meant by the term chain of command.
4. Suggest a reason why a matrix structure may be formed.
5. Explain what is meant by decentralisation.

Aspects of Organisation Structure

Formal and informal communication

An organisation structure shows the **formal** lines of communication that take place and the route that is taken for information and instructions to reach a particular place. Despite the existence of formal structures, **informal** structures (sometimes referred to as 'grapevines') can exist. Informal structures exist when communication takes place in ways that are not seen by looking at the formal structure.

Relationships in Organisations

Line relationships	These are between a subordinate and their superior. For example, a Marketing Manager has a line relationship with a Marketing Supervisor.
Lateral relationships	These are relationships between people on the same level of the organisation structure. A Human Resources Manager has a lateral relationship with the Operations Manager.
Functional relationships	These exist when one department provides support or a service to another department. The Human Resources department, for example, has a functional relationship with other departments when they provide support during the recruitment and selection process.

Organisation culture

Values, beliefs and norms related to the organisation that is shared by all its members.

This is sometimes referred to as **corporate culture**. It consists of **everything to do with the organisation** including its values, emotions, beliefs and language used. It is also to do with the attitude and behaviours that members of the organisation adopt because of the culture within the organisation. It is established from the beginning of the organisation's life and reflects the different activities (work and non-work related), policies and procedures that the organisation has. For example, does the organisation reward hard working staff? Does it provide opportunities for employees to socialise and work together?

The benefits of having a strong corporate culture are:
- Employees feel they belong to the organisation.
- It can motivate staff which in turn can improve efficiency and productivity.
- Positive relationships can be created and maintained.
- Employee loyalty can be increased.
- It can improve the image and identity of the organisation.

Changing the structure

Organisations may decide to restructure for a number of reasons, but mainly do so to keep up with the changing business environment. Over recent years, there has been a decline in manufacturing in the UK due to increase in foreign competition, changes in consumer demand and changes in government policies. Organisations must respond to changes in the business environment and, where necessary, change their organisation structure to suit the current business climate. The management of an organisation have the responsibility to ensure that the structure of the organisation meets its purpose.

Organisations can change the structure by **delayering** or **downsizing**.
Delayering means changing from a tall (or hierarchical structure) to a flat one by removing various levels (or layers) of management. Delayering allows for quicker communication, quicker decision making and can allow the organisation to adapt to changing market conditions when necessary. Staff can feel **empowered** to make their own decisions and use their own initiative, which in turn can increase their motivation and productivity. This is because managers have a wider **span of control**. Delayering will allow the organisation to save money on the salaries of managers.

Top Tip

Many candidates get the difference between delayering and downsizing wrong in their exam. Make sure this doesn't happen to you!

Delayering
Removing management levels to create a flatter structure.

Organisations can also change its structure by **downsizing**. This requires the organisation to remove some of its activities from its structure, for example a branch, factory or division. It may reduce the scale of its operations because of a decrease in demand. Some activities maybe **outsourced** to another organisation to enable the organisation to concentrate on its core activities. The organisation carrying out the activity on behalf of an organisation will be paid for doing this and this could be expensive. It also means that the organisation needs to trust the outsourced organisation to deliver on time and to the standard required. Effective communication between the two organisations is crucial to the success of outsourcing.

Sample examination questions

1. Explain what is meant by a 'matrix structure'. (2 marks)
2. Discuss the effects of outsourcing on an organisation. (5 marks)
3. Discuss the effects of widening the span of control. (7 marks)
4. Describe the benefits to an organisation of having a strong corporate culture. (3 marks)

Outsourcing	Span of control	Matrix structure	Functional relationships
Line relationships	Chain of command	Responsibility	Empower
Delayering	Entrepreneurial structure	Subordinate	Delegation
Authority	Downsizing	Activity groupings	Corporate culture

Congratulations

Congratulations on reaching the end of Unit 1: Business Enterprise! This is a good opportunity for you to review what you have learned during the unit, and ask your teacher/lecturer for help on anything you do not understand. Make sure you complete the section on 'Tracking Your Learning Journey'. Remember, the NAB for Unit 1 **will not** include the section on Internal Organisation, but your prelim and final exam might!

Quick Test 17

1. What is an informal structure?
2. Describe what is meant by corporate culture.
3. Describe what is meant by delayering.
4. Suggest two advantages of delayering.
5. Explain what outsourcing is.

What is Marketing?

Marketing is more than just advertising or selling a product. Marketing is about linking what to produce to what is consumed to ensure that the organisation meets the demands, needs and wants of customers in a market. A **market** consists of buyers and sellers who come together; customers give the organisation money in return for the organisation's product.

Organisations carry out a range of **marketing activities** including new product development, market research, deciding what to sell, what to charge and where to sell. They do these (and spend lots of money on it) for the reasons opposite.	■ To achieve the organisation's objectives ■ To raise product awareness ■ To obtain customers in new markets ■ To inform customers about the product ■ To estimate and determine what customers want

These marketing activities must be planned and carefully carried out in order to help the organisation achieve its objectives of, for example, increasing market share/growth or sales maximisation. A SWOT analysis may help in this process because the marketing function must consider the internal and external business environment (PESTEC factors) and the impact of this upon its marketing activities. Marketing is referred to as a strategic activity because it impacts upon the whole organisation and its vision.

Organisations can sell their products directly to consumers or to other organisations which will use them in their own production process. Goods sold for the purpose of being used at a later production stage are referred to as capital goods which are sold in industrial rather than consumer markets. Organisations will produce goods because they think they are good at it doing it and because they think the market will want it **(product orientated or product led)** or because they have carried out market research and have identified an opportunity to satisfy the needs of the customer **(market/customer orientated or market led)**.

Marketing <u>identifies</u> what customer wants, <u>anticipates</u> the customer's requirements and then attempts to <u>satisfy</u> these requirements.

- Marketing occurs in all organisations regardless of whether they belong to the private, public or voluntary sector.
- Between the organisation's objectives, decision making and its marketing activities.

Marketing mix

The **marketing mix** consists of the **4 Ps**. These are **product, price, place** and **promotion**. Organisations must get the balance between different elements of the marketing mix correct in order to be successful. Think of it like baking a cake; you need the correct quantities of each ingredient before your cake will turn out the way it should and successful marketing needs the correct quantities of each P. Each element is related to each other because, for example (i) the price charged needs to reflect the product sold, (ii) the product being sold can determine where and how it is sold. Changing one element of the marketing mix can also impact upon the other elements.

	Description	Importance
Product	This is the actual item (good or service) the organisation produces and sells.	Selling the correct product is crucial; customers won't buy something they do not want. The organisation must carry out **market research** to identify what customers want. The more products an organisation sells, the better chance they have of maximising sales.

Price	This is how much an organisation charges for each product.	The price of the product must reflect its quality and the demand for it but at the same time, allow the organisation to cover its costs and make a profit. It must not be too low or too high in comparison to the price of competitors.
Place	This is the way that the organisation gets the product to the customer and where it is sold. For example, a product may be sold in a shop, online or by telephone.	Customers need to be able to access the product; place ensures the product is available to customers in the most accessible place. Organisations sell their products in various places including shops, internet websites, mail order catalogues and on television.
Promotion	This is how the customer is made aware of the product and the ways they are encouraged to buy it. It consists of more than just advertising and includes other forms of promotion and other public relations.	Customers need to be aware that a product exists and why they should buy it. Organisations use promotion to encourage customers to buy a product. Please remember that promotion is more than just advertising.

Target markets

We have already seen that some organisations group their activities by customer type but not all do. Regardless of activity grouping, organisations may market their products towards a particular target market (**differentiated marketing**) or more than one target market (ie the whole population) or, in other words, **undifferentiated marketing**. If the organisation focuses on satisfying wants from a gap they have identified, this is known as a **niche market.** This is because it will be a specialised product or a product with limited demand and there will be very little competition in that market. Focusing marketing activities on particular market segments can have its benefits:

- Specific market segments can have products tailored to requirements.
- Prices can be set to reflect the market segment.
- It prevents money being wasted on promoting products to the wrong market segment.
- Products can be sold in the most appropriate place for the market segment.

The market can be segmented in some of the following ways:

Gender	Some products are marketed towards only men or women. *Eg certain perfumes are focused towards only men or only women.*
Age	Some products are marketed towards people in different age groups. *Eg some holiday packages and destinations are marketed towards the 18–30 age group.*
Income/ social class	Some products are marketed towards people who have high incomes. *Eg luxury sports cars or holidays.*
Religious belief	Some products are marketed towards people who have specific religious or cultural beliefs. *Eg particular clothing or food.*
Geographical location	Some products are marketed towards people who live in particular locations. *Eg fur coats for people who live in particularly cold countries!*

The Marketing Mix – Product

New product development

Before a product can be launched onto the market, the organisation will have carried out a number of tasks. These include:

- Carrying out market research to create a list of possible new products
- Discussing and thinking about each new possible product carefully and whether or not it has the finance and resources available to produce it
- Producing a prototype (a model) of what the finished product would look like
- Testing the market's reaction to the new product
- Promoting and advertising the product before it is launched.

Product life cycle

The product life cycle shows the various stages of a product's life.

During the **development** stage, the organisation will carry out the new product development activities listed above and then (hopefully!) the product is **introduced** to the market. During introduction, the product will be advertised and promoted heavily and sales will slowly increase. After it has been introduced, sales will begin **to grow** rapidly as customers have greater awareness of the product. The product will begin to make a profit for the organisation. When the product reaches **maturity**, sales have reached its peak and the product is profitable. So that the organisation can continue to make high profits and to eliminate competition, extension strategies will be introduced with the aim of keeping the product in this stage for as long as possible. When sales begin to fall the product has entered the **decline** stage and will eventually become obsolete from the market.

Organisations will use a range of **extension strategies** in order to keep the product in the maturity stage for as long as possible. Extension strategies aim to inject new life into the product and make it appeal to customers for as long as possible. These may include:

Changing the product's use, changing the packaging, improving the product by adding new features or varieties, changing the name of the product, changing methods of promotion or changing the product's price.

Top Tip

Always give examples where you can on each extension strategy. For example, do not just write 'improve product' – you must say how, eg add a new feature or introduce a new variety.

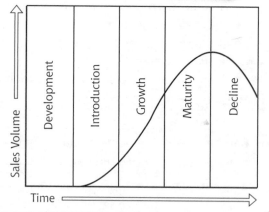

Product mix

Many organisations sell more than one product in order to minimise risk, appeal to a variety of market segments and to increase the chances of sales and profit maximisation. The range of products that an organisation sells is called the **product mix** or **product portfolio**. The range of products that an organisation sells will usually be marketed towards a variety of market segments. The range of products the organisation sells can be looked at on the **Boston Matrix** (or Boston Box). Each product is placed on the Boston Matrix with the aim of as having many 'stars' as possible. Organisations will plan their marketing activities to attempt to achieve this.

Do not confuse the product mix with the marketing mix. They are different!

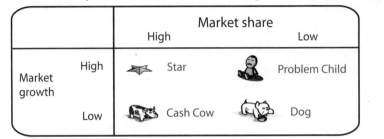

Branding

The name, symbol or logo given to a group or type of product is known as its brand. A brand makes one product or group of products different from other competitor products. Examples of common brands are Cadburys, McDonalds and Heinz.

Advantages of brands	Disadvantages of brands
■ Brand loyalty can be established ■ Often associated with quality ■ Higher prices can be charged ■ Brands are easily and quickly recognised ■ New products with the brand name can be introduced successfully	■ Poor brands can have serious consequences; customers may associate the whole product range with poor quality ■ Can be copied or fakes produced ■ Time consuming and expensive to establish a brand identity

Some businesses have **own brand** products which means they have that business' name on them, but are usually manufactured by other companies.

Advantages of own brands	Disadvantages of own brands
■ Do not require much advertising ■ Usually cheaper than other branded products which can make them popular with customers (seen as 'value for money') ■ Manufactured by other companies but the business retains control over the production process	■ Sometimes seen as being of a poorer quality compared to other brands ■ Can be viewed as just a copy or imitation of other brands

Sample examination questions

1. Explain how extension strategies can prolong the life of a product. (6 marks)
2. Organisations spend vast sums of money developing new products. Describe the stages that take place before a new product is launched onto the market. (6 marks)
3. Discuss the advantages and disadvantages to organisations such as ASDA of selling own brand products. (4 marks)

Quick Test 18

1. What is the product life cycle?
2. Identify five stages of the product life cycle.
3. What does the Boston Matrix show?
4. Suggest two advantages of branding.
5. Suggest two advantages of own brands.

The Marketing Mix – Price

The price of the product is very important, especially when introducing a new product to the market or when attempting to extend the life cycle of a product. Organisations have various factors to consider when setting a product's price.

Pricing: Factors to be Considered

- How much can be supplied.
- How unique the product is
- The product's target market/market segment
- How much profit is wanted

- Costs to make the product
- How much competitors are charging
- The product's life cycle position

Pricing strategies

Organisations use different pricing strategies to achieve different objectives. Some pricing strategies are used to attract customers while other ones are used to give a product an exclusive image.

Strategy	Description	Justification
Competitive pricing	The product's price is similar to competitors.	Attracts customers and allows businesses to compete with other businesses who sell a similar product.
Penetration (introductory) pricing	The product's price is set low in order to increase market share. It is used when a product is initially launched.	This strategy will allow a business to attract customers from their competitors.
Market skimming	A high price is charged for a new and often unique product.	A high price can be charged due to no or little competition and because of the uniqueness of the product. A large profit can be made. The price can be lowered at a later date if competition enters the market.
Premium pricing	High prices are charged for the product.	The high price gives the product a unique and exclusive image.
Destroyer pricing	The product's price is set intentionally low.	This strategy is used to force competitors out of the market so that higher prices can be charged later. It attracts customers.
Promotional pricing	Price of the product is low in the short term, eg 25% off this week only.	Customers who buy on impulse will often take advantage of these offers. It can also be used to reduce stock levels.
Loss leaders	Selling the product at a price lower than it costs to make it.	Attracts customers to the business, who will hopefully purchase other products that are priced normally. The business will make a profit based on the overall cost to the customer of the products purchased.
Psychological pricing	This involves setting a price that makes customers think the product is cheaper than it actually is, eg 99p rather than £1 or £1·99 rather than £2.	Customers are attracted because they think the product is cheaper than it actually is.

Top Tip

It is important you are able to identify, describe and justify different pricing strategies.

Which price?

Businesses need to think carefully about which price to charge. Certain pricing strategies are only to be used in the short term, some are only for exclusive items and some can be used in the long term.

Market skimming and premium pricing, for example, can be used as strategies for unique and exclusive products. This is because these strategies demand a higher price. In competitive markets, competitive pricing or destroyer pricing could be used in the hope it will remove competition from the market.

Some organisations can charge high prices because other factors will contribute to their success, eg uniqueness of the product, little competition in the market, brand loyalty or because there is a limited supply of the product.

Organisations constantly review the prices they charge because they operate in an environment that does not stand still. Changes in demand because of changes in lifestyle and social trends are common as are pressures from customers for lower prices. Competitors are also doing their market research and trying to introduce products that will be better and cheaper than their rivals.

Top Tip

Look carefully at past paper questions to see the types of questions on price. Quite often they will ask you to justify why certain strategies should be used in certain situations, eg high prices for exclusive products.

> Between the price of a product and the external business environment – PESTEC factors.

Sample examination questions

1. Describe three pricing tactics that could be used when an organisation attempts to break into a new market. (6 marks)
2. Explain why firms use loss leaders as a pricing tactic. (3 marks)
3. Describe pricing strategies that could be used in a highly competitive market such as the mobile phone industry. (4 marks)
4. Describe four factors that allow organisations to remain successful while charging customers high prices. (4 marks)

Quick Test 19

1. What is price?
2. Identify two factors that will decide how much is charged for a product.
3. Describe what is meant by penetration pricing.
4. Describe what is meant by loss leader.
5. Suggest a reason why premium pricing might be used for exclusive products.

The Marketing Mix – Place

Place is about getting the product to the customer or, in other words, **distributing** a organisation's product. An organisation must ensure products reach the most appropriate customer in the correct quantities, at the correct time and through the best **channel of distribution**.

Channels of distribution

A channel of distribution is the route a product will follow to get from the manufacturer to the customer. It can take one of many routes as shown below. **Remember, the channel always starts with the manufacturer and ends with the customer** and this in itself is one way to distribute the product. However, there are others including the use of a **retailer** or **wholesaler**.

Top Tip

Channels of distribution and methods of transport are different. Write down the differences between them in your notes.

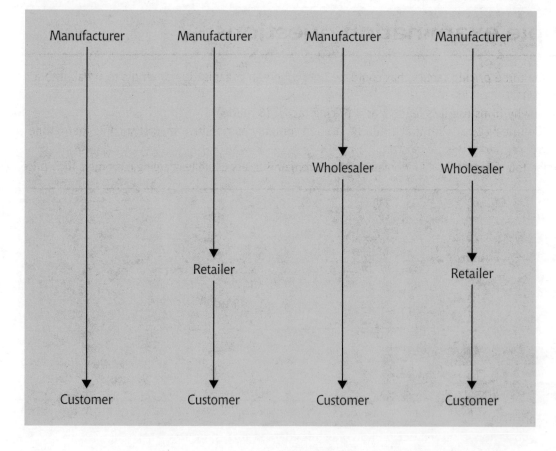

There are a number of factors that will determine which channel of distribution is used. These factors include:

- The actual product and its life cycle (products with a shorter life cycle may need to be sold directly to the customer to preserve them).
- The image the manufacturer wants the product to have.
- Availability of finance.
- Reputation and reliability of wholesalers and retailers.
- Any legal restrictions.

How the product actually gets from the factory of the manufacturer to the customer depends on the chosen method of transport, eg road, rail, sea or air. This is known as the method of **physical distribution**.

Physical Distribution Methods

Method	Benefits	Costs
Road	▪ Relatively cheap compared to other methods ▪ Delivery can be fairly quick ▪ Customer can have the product delivered directly to their door	▪ Larger items cannot be transported as easily ▪ Less green and environmentally friendly ▪ Can be roadworks and delays
Rail	▪ Large products and fairly large quantities can be transported	▪ Rail links are not available in every location
Air	▪ Products can be transported across the world fairly quickly compared, eg to sea ▪ Large amounts of small products can be distributed	▪ Products still need to be transported to an airport which could be expensive ▪ Large items cannot be transported
Sea	▪ Larger products can be distributed ▪ Products can be distributed across the world	▪ It could take a long time for goods to arrive in far away destinations

Retailers and wholesalers

A **retailer** is an organisation that distributes products to the customer on behalf of the manufacturer. Retailers stock a range of products from a number of manufacturers and wholesalers. They will decide on the price to be charged to the customer and will display them in the most effective way to be sold. The manufacturer will decide which retailer to use based on where the customers are and what extra services (eg credit and delivery terms) they offer the customer. Retailers benefit from sourcing products directly from a manufacturer in terms of being able to specify exactly they want and at what cost, and sometimes the retailer can take advantage of **economies of scale**. However, sometimes manufacturers will not use a retailer in the distribution channel because the product will face competition in the retailer's store and because it adds on an extra financial cost to the distribution channel.

A **wholesaler** buys large quantities of items from the manufacturer and then sells them on to retailers (or sometimes directly to the customer) in smaller quantities. Many larger retailers do not use a wholesaler as part of their distribution channel because they have their own warehouses and transport systems.

The use of a wholesaler offers many benefits to both the manufacturer and to a retailer:

Benefits to the manufacturer	Benefits to the retailer
<ul><li>Distribution and storage costs are cut because the wholesaler will buy and store stock in bulk.</li><li>The wholesaler may promote the manufactured product.</li><li>Risk of not selling the product to a retailer or to customers is taken on by the wholesaler.</li><li>Packaging, labelling and marketing of the product may be done by the wholesaler.</li></ul>	<ul><li>Information on the product may be provided by the wholesaler.</li><li>Smaller retailers might be able to take advantage of credit facilities and delivery terms.</li><li>They do not have to pay for expensive storage facilities because the wholesaler will sell smaller quantities to the retailer compared to obtaining the product directly from the manufacturer.</li></ul>

Direct selling

Internet selling	This method involves selling products to the customer through an internet website. See the section on ICT (page 28) and promotion (page 56) for more information on internet selling and websites. Organisations can target customers worldwide through internet selling and can do this 24/7. Customers are often able to take advantage of online discounts as well as accessing up-to-date product information and availability. Some internet websites can allow customers to compare products.
Direct mail	This involves posting letters or leaflets directly to the homes and offices of potential customers.

Benefits	Costs
■ Specific market segments can be targeted ■ Wide geographical areas can be targeted	■ Customers may not appreciate receiving lots of mail in this way ('junk' mail) and may not even open it

Mail order	This is when catalogues are used to sell products.

Benefits	Costs
■ Convenient to the customer as they can browse through the catalogue at their own pace and order when they feel ready ■ No need for expensive stores on the High Street	■ Expensive to produce catalogues and to promote ■ No personal service ■ Delivery times ■ Can only see goods in a catalogue and they may need to be sent back if unwanted or unsuitable

Top Tip

Remember, there are costs and benefits of direct selling not just to the customer but also to the organisation.

Quick Test 20

1. Explain what is meant by a channel of distribution.
2. Describe what is meant by a retailer.
3. Describe what is meant by a wholesaler.
4. Identify three methods of direct selling.
5. Suggest a benefit to the customer of direct selling through an internet website.

The Marketing Mix – Promotion

Promotion describes the different methods an organisation uses to make customers aware that a product exists and also the ways they are encouraged to buy it. It consists of more than just **advertising** and includes other forms of promotion (**into the pipeline** and **out of the pipeline**), and **public relations**.

Advertising

Advertising communicates that a product exists. It usually includes information about the product and, at the same time, tries to encourage customers to buy it. Advertising helps to increase sales because if customers don't know that a product exists, they can't buy it.

| **Internet websites** | An internet website is a collection of information in one place which can be seen by typing in a website address (URL) into a program such as Internet Explorer. An organisation may have a website to communicate information about its products and also to sell products online; this is known as e-commerce. |

Top Tip

There are advantages and disadvantages to the **customer** and to the **organisation** of selling online.

Advantages

- Customers worldwide can be targeted.
- Customers can buy online 24/7 from a place of their choice.
- Online discounts are often given.
- Product information can be updated and accessed quickly.
- Products can be compared with others.
- Easy to use if transport is not available to the retailer.
- Stock availability can be checked and items reserved before purchasing.
- The organisation can set up a website fairly cheaply.

Disadvantages

- Customer is unable to handle or see the goods fully.
- Customers may be unwilling to leave their personal or credit/debit card details.
- There may be computer or internet problems while ordering.
- It can take some time for items to arrive.
- Items may get lost or damaged during delivery, or they could go out-of-date.
- The customer may find it difficult to find their way around a website.
- The customer has no personal contact with the organisation.

Top Tip

Exam questions on the use of an internet website to sell and market products have been common in recent years.

A variety of things can be done to encourage people to buy online. These include offering discounts, free postage, fast delivery times and having a website that is easy to use and that offers secure payment facilities. Organisations can use sound, graphics and video clips to make their website more appealing and attractive. Allowing customers to search for information on the site, a 'Contact Us' facility and Frequently Asked Question (FAQs) section are also useful.

Newspapers	Several types of newspapers are available; some are only available locally and some are only available on a Sunday. There are several newspapers that are designed for specific audiences (eg the Financial Times for those with an interest in business).	
	Advantages	**Disadvantages**
	■ National newspapers allow for an audience across the country, whereas local newspapers target people in a particular location. ■ Adverts can be kept by readers for use at a later date. ■ Depending on the advert size, a lot of information can be communicated.	■ Some newspapers do not print everything in colour; this may have less of an impact. ■ No sound or video clips can be shown to show how the product would function. ■ Could be expensive to advertise in (eg national) newspapers.

Television	Television advertising has the potential to reach a large audience because many people watch television. Adverts are only shown on certain channels and between different programmes or during commercial breaks.	
	Advantages	**Disadvantages**
	■ Large audiences can be reached. ■ Adverts can be shown during particular programmes to target specific audiences to whom the product may most appeal. ■ The product can be shown from different viewpoints and demonstrations given which are in colour.	■ Advertising nationally on TV could be expensive. ■ Some people tend not to watch the adverts and instead turn over to another programme. ■ As adverts tend to be very short, people do not have much time to take in the advert and take note of all the product details or contact information.

Media publicity	The media sometimes report on the positive and negative activities of organisations in their news reports or broadcasts.	
	Advantages	**Disadvantages**
	■ Free advertising for the organisation provided it is a positive media report. ■ If the media is national (eg national newspaper or news broadcast) a large audience could see it.	■ The activities being reported on may not be positive; this could have a negative impact upon the organisation and its sales. ■ The media might not report the whole situation; facts could be misleading or interpreted in a way unintended.

There are other methods of advertising that can be used. Organisations are taking advantage of modern technology (eg text messaging) to promote their products as well as more traditional methods such as direct mail, radio and billboards.

Organisations often pay celebrities to promote their product to the public. This is known as **product endorsement**. David Beckham, for example, has been the face of Pepsi and Jamie Oliver endorses Sainsburys.

Advantages	Disadvantages
■ Promotes a good image/name for the organisation. ■ People often want to buy products to be associated with the celebrity. ■ If the celebrity is successful, sales levels can be increased.	■ Highly expensive. ■ The correct celebrity needs to be chosen to match the image the product should have. ■ Any negative publicity about the celebrity can impact upon sales of the product.

Marketing

The **Advertising Standards Authority** monitors advertising and other forms of promotion to ensure they are to the required standard. They also investigate any advertising related complaints. They have the authority to have adverts or promotions changed if they contain wrong information.

Pressure groups have an aim of trying to influence an organisation. They make take action to try to force an organisation to take a particular course of action or to make a particular decision. A pressure group will be more effective in its aims if it is well organised, is sufficiently financed, is persistent and receives significant press coverage.

Pipeline promotions

MANUFACTURER → Into the pipeline → **RETAILER** → Out of the pipeline → **CUSTOMER**

Into the pipeline
Manufacturers encourage retailers to stock their products

eg point of sale materials, dealer loaders, sale or return, dealer competitions, staff training, credit facilities

Out of the pipeline
Retailers encourage customers to buy

eg free samples, loyalty schemes, credit facilities, demonstrations, competitions, offers (BOGOF, etc), vouchers

Top Tip

It is important you understand the difference between into the pipeline and out of the pipeline promotions and are able to describe the different methods used.

Into the pipeline promotions	Out of the pipeline promotions
Point of sale materials Often free posters, display stands and other material are given to retailers to display products to customers.	**Free samples** Customers are given small samples of the product free of charge so that they can see/test the product in the hope they will buy it (eg food or drink tasting in supermarkets).
Sale or return The manufacturer gives the retailer the opportunity to return any untried products to reduce the risk of being left with stock that has not sold.	**Loyalty schemes** Many larger retailers offer loyalty schemes to customers whereby they collect points for making purchases. These points can then be used to obtain vouchers for discount on future purchases or for free admission/discounts on popular visitor attractions.
Staff training The manufacturer may provide training and demonstrations to the retailer's staff so that they feel confident in promoting the manufacturer's product.	**Vouchers** These are usually given in newspapers/magazines or in store. They entitle the customer to a discount on purchases they make at a later date.
Dealer (retailer) loaders These are offers given to encourage retailers to stock the manufacturer's products (eg buy so many and get one free).	**Special offers** For example, Buy One Get One Free (BOGOF), buy two get the third free and other reductions in the price of products. They are usually short term and only on selected products.

Descriptions of the other into the pipeline and out of the pipeline promotions can be found in the Course Notes.

Public relations

Public relations (PR) attempts to improve the relationship and communication between the general public and an organisation. The key difference between PR and advertising is that PR is not paid for. Large organisations may have a PR office or department who would be responsible for organising PR activities. Good public relations will give the organisation a good image which in turn may increase sales, but negative publicity would do the opposite. PR activities an organisation has may include:

Top Tip

Remember – advertising is only one part of promotion.

Press releases	A press release is usually a written statement to the press (eg newspapers and TV stations) that communicate the activities within the organisation.
Sponsorships	Organisations may sponsor events where there is likely to be a lot of public attention. Sports and charity events are often sponsored by large organisations which have their company name displayed on material that the sport or charity is distributing. Organisations support these types of events because it promotes their image which in turn will hopefully increase sales.
Charity donations	Organisations may donate sums of money to charities in the hope not only of helping a good cause, but because they will receive good publicity from it. This in turn raises awareness of the organisation and will hopefully increase sales.

In the event of the organisation receiving bad publicity it would be the responsibility of the PR office or department to respond to such publicity. It may do this by issuing a press release with the viewpoint and stance of the organisation.

Sample examination questions

1. Describe the methods available to a public relations department to improve the image of an organisation. (5 marks)
2. Describe the benefits of using the internet to market products. (5 marks)
3. Describe the factors affecting an organisation's choice of channel of distribution. (7 marks)

Quick Test 21

1. Describe the term promotion.
2. Suggest a problem the customer may have when purchasing online.
3. Describe the term product endorsement.
4. Suggest three methods of into the pipeline promotion.
5. Explain what is meant by public relations.
6. Describe the term press release.

Market Research

Businesses operate in a market and market research aims to find out information about what is happening within that market. It will involve the business having to actively research and record what is going on in the market as well as carefully looking at information that already exists.

Market research can tell the organisation a huge amount about what is going on in the market. It can tell them:

- Information about the types of customers that are making purchases
- How good its marketing and promotion techniques are
- How customers have reacted to its products, prices and promotions
- What customers would like to see in the future; where it can develop new products to meet customers wants.

Businesses carry out market research for the above reasons, and to try to keep ahead of their competitors. A business needs to keep up with what customers want and ensure its product, price, place and promotion are all appropriate for the market segment.

There are two main types of market research – **desk** and **field**.

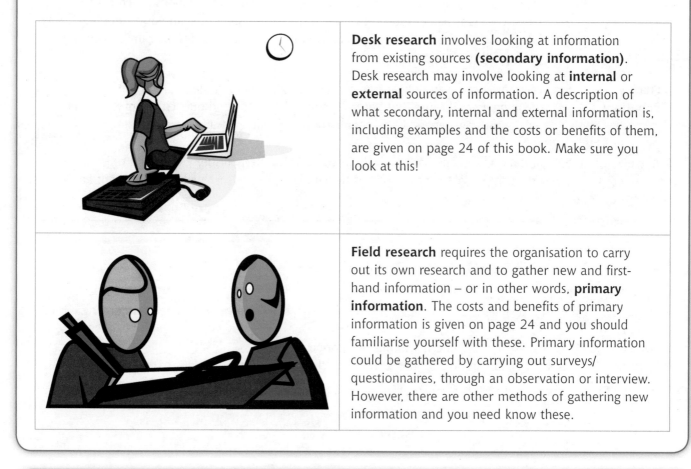

Desk research involves looking at information from existing sources **(secondary information)**. Desk research may involve looking at **internal** or **external** sources of information. A description of what secondary, internal and external information is, including examples and the costs or benefits of them, are given on page 24 of this book. Make sure you look at this!

Field research requires the organisation to carry out its own research and to gather new and first-hand information – or in other words, **primary information**. The costs and benefits of primary information is given on page 24 and you should familiarise yourself with these. Primary information could be gathered by carrying out surveys/ questionnaires, through an observation or interview. However, there are other methods of gathering new information and you need know these.

Surveys

A survey (or questionnaire) involves asking people their views and opinions on issues by asking them a series of questions. It could be done in person, over the telephone or though the post. Sometimes people might be asked for their general views or they might be asked to rate certain things, eg on a scale of 1–5 rate how much they agree or disagree with certain things.

Postal survey – this is when people will be sent a questionnaire through the post. They will be asked to complete it and then send it back to the organisation.

Advantages	Disadvantages
■ Large numbers of people spread across a large geographical area can be surveyed at a fairly inexpensive cost. ■ Larger surveys can be carried out and people can complete them at their own pace at a time and place of their choosing.	■ Relies on people opening the letter containing the questionnaire, completing it and then sending it back; not many people do this. ■ Information is not obtained instantly. ■ The respondent does not have the opportunity to clarify anything he or she does not understand. ■ The survey must be designed carefully so that it is not open to interpretation or misunderstanding.

Telephone survey – this is when people will be contacted by telephone and asked to answer a series of questions.

Advantages	Disadvantages
■ Large numbers of people spread across a large area can be surveyed. ■ Less expensive to conduct compared to a personal interview. ■ The person being surveyed has the opportunity to clarify anything he or she is not sure of. ■ Information is obtained instantly.	■ Many people do not like taking part in telephone surveys and may not do so. ■ Large and time consuming surveys are unlikely to go down well and therefore this method tends to only suit short surveys.

Top Tip

Remember – surveys and questionnaires are the same thing.

Personal interview – this involves a face-to-face two-way process whereby a researcher (the interviewer) will ask a person a number of questions and he or she will respond orally with their answer.

Advantages	Disadvantages
■ The researcher or person being interviewed can clarify anything he or she does not understand.	■ Time consuming and expensive to carry out; not many people can be asked for their opinions in this way compared to a postal or telephone survey. ■ The researcher will require training in interview and questioning techniques for it to be successful.

Focus groups

A focus group is simply a discussion between a selected number of people and an experienced researcher. People will be asked for their views (qualitative information) on certain things and the idea is to generate a discussion on these.

Advantages	Disadvantages
■ Peoples feelings and views can be gained.	■ Qualitative information is difficult to analyse.

Marketing

Hall test

A Hall test involves a product being given to customers to try to then obtain their opinions and views (qualitative information) on it; they are basically being given a free trial of the product.

Advantages	Disadvantages
■ Customers get to try out the product for themselves and can report back on it. ■ Fairly inexpensive to carry out.	■ Qualitative information is difficult to analyse. ■ Customer may give the response they think the organisation wants to hear as they do not want to appear rude or ungrateful.

Observation

An observation involves watching something and recording what happens. It could be that the observer has to count how many times something happens, someone does something (gathering quantitative information) or what someone's reaction is to a particular situation.

Advantages	Disadvantages
■ Quantitative information is gathered which is easier to analyse compared to qualitative. ■ Those being observed may be unaware so are responding to the situation in a natural way.	■ Those being observed cannot be asked their opinion or give an explanation as to why they did or did not do something.

Other methods of field research you may wish to investigate include consumer audits, EPOS and test marketing.

Top Tip

Spend time learning about the different methods of field research and their advantages/disadvantages. Look at past paper questions to see the types of questions that have been asked previously (and the marks they are worth!).

Sampling

When organisations carry out field research, it is impossible for them to ask everyone for their opinion on something. For this reason, they have to select which people to question or, in other words, select a sample of people to be questioned. There are different ways of creating a sample to be questioned, including:

- **Random sampling** – randomly selecting people from a list, eg telephone book or electoral roll, and then telephoning these people. People who are chosen from the list to take part in the survey must be contacted – even if it takes several attempts!
- **Stratified random sampling** – the sample is based on segments of how the population as a whole is divided.
- **Quota sampling** – selecting a number of people to question based on certain characteristics (eg age, occupation, gender).

Sample examination questions

1. Describe four methods of field research. (8 marks)
2. Explain why organisations choose to spend large sums of money on marketing. (5 marks)
3. Explain the various means of sampling that could be used to obtain a cross-section of views when carrying out market research. (4 marks)
4. Describe the advantages and disadvantages of three types of field research an organisation could use to obtain primary information. (8 marks)

Marketing mix	Product portfolio	Branding	Direct selling
Sampling	Market research	Survey	Boston Matrix
Field research	Desk research	Channel of distribution	Product
Into the pipeline	Pressure groups	Out of the pipeline	Retailer
Wholesaler	Market segments	Product life cycle	Price
Extension strategies	Place	Advertising	Public relations
Product endorsement	Market led	Product mix	Promotion
Pricing strategies	Product led	Niche marketing	

Quick Test 22

1. Identify the two types of market research.
2. Explain the difference between the two types of market research.
3. Identify three types of surveys that could be carried out.
4. Describe what is meant by a focus group.
5. What is a sample?

Role and Importance of Operations

The operations function in an organisation is concerned with making goods and providing services by turning inputs into outputs. This is essential to enable the organisation to make profit and create wealth. Operations is important because it is one of an organisation's core activities.

Managing the operations function is important to ensure that products are of a quality that will generate income and to keep wastage to a minimum. Wastage can be very costly to an organisation.

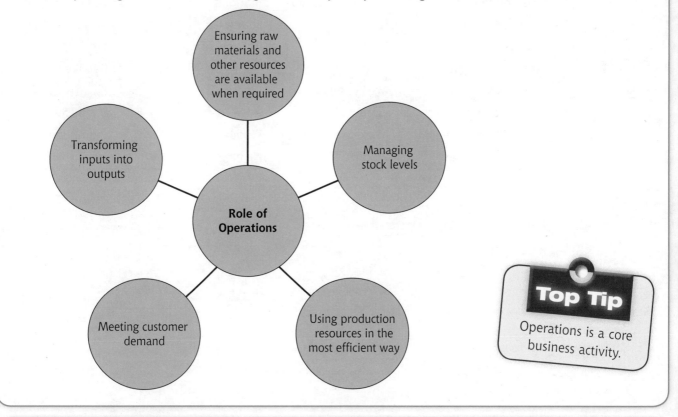

Top Tip

Operations is a core business activity.

Operating system

Operations transforms inputs into outputs. This is done by deciding the best way to transform raw materials and other inputs into the finished product and at the same time organising the necessary resources to do this. This is called the **operating system**. At all times, it is important to remember that the quality of the finished product is very important and every step needs to be taken to ensure it.

INPUTS ⟹	PROCESS ⟹	OUTPUTS
Factors of production	Production processes, Quality checks	The finished product

We can categorise the activities of operations into three areas. Each will be considered in turn on the following pages.

1	The purchase and storage of raw materials
2	The production and storage of finished goods
3	The distribution of the finished goods

Purchasing of raw materials

Raw materials are an essential ingredient in any production process because without them products could not be made.

Top Tip

Make sure you have learned the factors to be considered when choosing a supplier of raw materials and the reasons why those factors are important (the justifications).

When a business is **deciding upon a supplier to use** and **how much raw material to purchase**, it must consider the questions below. The factors that need to be considered are known as the **purchasing mix**.

	Reasons why it is important
What is the best price available?	■ Costs need to be kept at a minimum to maximise profit. ■ Low costs contribute to a healthy cash flow.
Of what quality are the raw materials to be supplied?	■ Without quality raw materials, the finished product will not be of an acceptable quality. ■ Quality needs to be consistent because the finished product needs to be of a consistent quality for the customer. ■ To keep wastage to a minimum.
How reliable and dependable is the supplier?	■ It could be costly to the business if the supplier did not deliver on time; production would need to stop and customers would not be happy if delivery times were not met.
How long will it take for the raw materials to be delivered?	■ Some raw materials may be perishable and therefore would be required quickly to be used in production. ■ The business does not want production to stop because it is costly and delivery deadlines might not be met.

Like any other input, we need to ensure they are of a suitable quality; if we don't have quality inputs then we can't expect our finished product to be of quality!

Operations

What quantity is required?	■ There should always be enough raw materials available at any one time to allow production to continue. However, too much will mean that it is required to be stored, which could be expensive. ■ Quantity should never go above the maximum stock level.
What storage space is available?	■ Storage could be expensive and the business wants to keep costs low to maximise profit.

The business may ask other questions, such as what credit terms are offered and what discounts are available for bulk buying.

Payment systems

The operations function relies on appropriately skilled employees and in turn for their effort, they need to be paid. There are different systems which can be used to pay employees.

Time rate	Employees are paid per hour worked. The more hours worked by the employee the more pay they will receive. For example, if an employee works 20 hours per week at £7.00 per hour, they will receive £140.00 for their work (before payments for tax and national insurance is deducted).
Flat rate	Employees are paid a set amount per year which is divided into twelve equal monthly payments. This is also known as a salary. For example, if an employee is paid a £18,000 salary, they would receive 12 equal monthly payments of £1500 (before payments for tax and national insurance is deducted).
Piece rate	Employees are paid per item produced normally in addition to a low flat rate. For example, the flat rate might be £600 per month. In addition to this, they might receive £0.25 for every item produced. Organisations will vary in the flat rate that they pay as well as the piece rate that is offered. The product being manufactured will determine the amount of piece rate paid.
Overtime	After working a set number of hours, overtime is paid for the extra hours worked. Usually the amount paid per hour overtime is more than the normal hourly rate. It could be 'time and a half' or 'double-time'. For example, an employee normally works 35 hours at £7.00 per hour. If they were asked to work overtime (hours in addition to the 35 hours already worked), they might be paid time and a half, so therefore would receive £10.50 per hour of overtime worked.
Commission	The amount of commission an employee receives depends on the value of sales they have made. Commission is usually a % of the sales value the employee has made. It might be paid in addition to a flat rate amount or it might not.
Bonus	A bonus is an additional payment an employee might get having, eg. exceeded productivity targets. It will be paid in addition to their flat rate.
Fringe benefits	These are non-financial payments made usually to employees in professional or managerial positions. A fringe benefit could be a company car, private health care or free access to health and fitness facilities.

Sample examination questions

1. Discuss the importance of quality inputs in the operations process of an organisation. (4 marks)
2. Explain the factors that are important in selecting an appropriate supplier of raw materials for a restaurant. (5 marks)

Quick Test 23

1. What is the role of operations?
2. Why is operations important?
3. Explain what is meant by the term the 'purchasing mix'.
4. Suggest two reasons why choosing a reliable supplier is important.

Managing Stock, Warehouses and Distribution

The term stock refers to raw materials, goods that are currently being manufactured (work in progress) and finished goods. At all stages of the production process, stock must be managed because there must be sufficient quantities of raw materials and finished goods at all times.

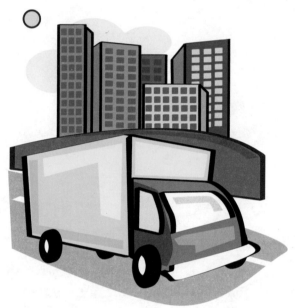

When manufacturing and storing goods there are certain issues to be considered:

- Demand for the finished product (how much is required?)
- How many products can be manufactured at one time?
- Working practices, procedures and health and safety requirements
- Storage facilities available
- Procedures for maintaining and managing quality.

Organisations need to calculate an **optimum** or **economic stock level**, which is the best quantity of stock at any one time. This ensures that costs are kept to a minimum as well as having enough stock to meet production and customer requirements at any one time.

Consequences of too little stock	Consequences of too much stock
▪ Production could stop ▪ Customers might not have their orders on time ▪ Poor reputation and image which could result in losing customers	▪ Financial costs (storage, security, insurance) ▪ Stock that could go to waste or deteriorate ▪ Risk of stock being stolen

Organisations need to have a system in place that manages levels of stock. They do this by setting a **maximum stock level, minimum stock level, re-order level** and **re-order quantity**.

Maximum stock level – the maximum amount of stock at any one time.

Minimum stock level – the minimum quantity of stock at any one time.

Re-order level – the quantity of stock at which more stock is ordered.

Re-order quantity – the quantity of stock to be ordered to bring levels back to the maximum stock level.

Managing Stock, Warehouses and Distribution

Any stock management system needs to take into account delivery times **(lead time)**. Remember, stock levels should never fall below the minimum level and this influences how much is required to be ordered. The diagram below illustrates stock management.

Top Tip

You should learn this diagram carefully. Be prepared to draw it and label it accordingly in a question on stock management. Properly drawn and labelled diagrams do attract marks!

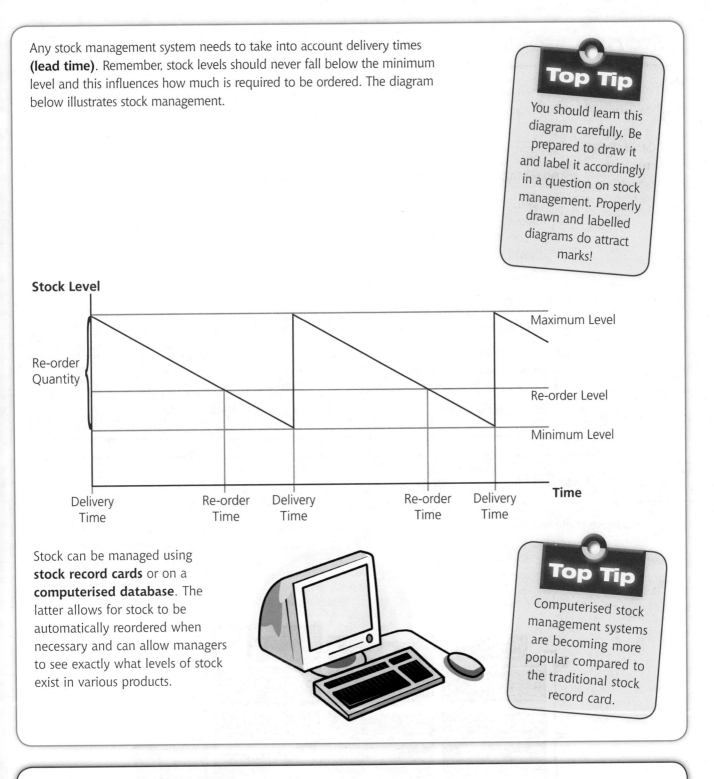

Stock can be managed using **stock record cards** or on a **computerised database**. The latter allows for stock to be automatically reordered when necessary and can allow managers to see exactly what levels of stock exist in various products.

Top Tip

Computerised stock management systems are becoming more popular compared to the traditional stock record card.

Just in Time (JIT)

Just in Time is a method of stock control that keeps stock levels to the minimum possible levels. As the name suggests, stock arrives *just in time* for them to be used in the production process and goods are only manufactured when a customer order is received. JIT in practice requires suppliers who can deliver on time otherwise production will stop and it also requires procedures in place to ensure quality is maintained. However, it does save money being tied up in stock as well as in the storage and security of stock. There is also less chance of stock going to waste through deterioration.

Storing stock

It may seem like an obvious question, but where is stock stored? It can be stored in a **centralised** location or a **decentralised** location.

Centralised storage	This means keeping stock in one place.	
	Advantages	**Disadvantages**
	■ Security is easier so therefore less theft is likely. ■ Procedures for receiving, issuing and distributing stock can be easier to implement across the whole organisation.	■ A dedicated area for storing stock could be expensive to set up and maintain. ■ Time could be wasted going to and from the storage area.
Decentralised storage	This means keeping stock in more than one place.	
	Advantages	**Disadvantages**
	■ Stock can be more easily accessed and can be obtained easily when needed. ■ Less chance of stock going to waste or deteriorating.	■ Storage space in several locations is required. ■ Security is more difficult to maintain so risk of theft is higher.

Warehousing

A **warehouse** is the name given to the place where finished products are held until ready to be distributed to the customer. Warehouses need to be designed to ensure the most efficient movement and flow of stock. The size and exact layout of a warehouse depends on the size of the organisation, the product being manufactured and the organisation's procedures.

Distribution

Distribution is concerned with getting the finished product to the right customer. We looked at channels of distribution earlier (see page 52) as well as methods of transportation (physical distribution). You need to revisit this section to remind yourself of these.

How the product gets to the customer depends on the **distribution mix.** The distribution mix identifies various factors to be considered when deciding upon the route to get the product to the customer.

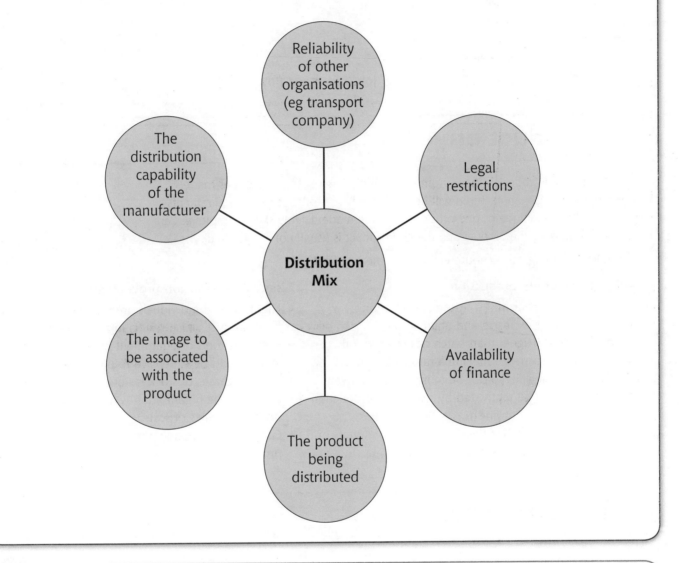

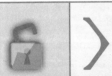 The organisation's ability to deliver the product on time to the customer could however be affected by factors outwith the organisation's control (external factors). You should review the section on external factors (see page 37) and consider how these could impact upon the organisation's ability to distribute its products.

Quick Test 24

1. Identify the three types of stock.
2. Describe what is meant by the optimum (economic) stock level.
3. Explain the difference between a centralised and decentralised stock storage area.
4. Explain what is meant by the distribution mix.

Production Methods

Organisations must decide which method or methods of production to use to create their product or in other words, how to **process** the **inputs** into **outputs**.

In deciding which method would be best used, there are several issues to be considered:

- Type and nature of the product being made
- Amount of the product to be manufactured
- Methods of monitoring and ensuring quality
- Method of distribution
- Stock control management system
- Resources and technology available

There are three main methods of production: **job, batch** and **flow.**

Top Tip

Remember – value is being added and wealth created as products move from one part of the production process to another.

Job production

This is when one product is made from start to finish before another one is made. The product being manufactured will be made to the customer's exact requirements which results in a unique or one-off product being made. Highly skilled employees are involved in making the product and the end product is usually of a high quality.

Examples: wedding cakes, house extensions, pieces of art.

Advantages of job production	Disadvantages of job production
■ The exact demands of the customer can be met. ■ High prices for exclusive and unique products can be commanded. (Higher than batch or flow methods.) ■ Employees experience making a range of products using different skills so can be more highly motivated. ■ Employees can be motivated by seeing the production process from start to finish. ■ It is possible to change the design or requirements of the product even when production has begun.	■ Highly skilled individuals are required to make each product which results in a high wages bill. ■ Specialist tools or equipment may be necessary which could be expensive to purchase. ■ Bulk purchases of stock is not always possible therefore the organisation is not benefiting from economies of scale. ■ Can take considerable time to manufacture products.

Batch production

This is when one batch of identical products is made at a time, before another batch of different products is made. All products in the batch move on to each stage of production at the same time. Machinery and equipment may be cleaned and/or changed in between batches to produce a different product. Batch production is used when manufacturing a product that comes in different varieties, styles or sizes.

Examples: clothing, newspapers, bread.

Advantages of batch production	Disadvantages of batch production
■ Batches can be changed to suit the requirements and demands of the customer (therefore there is some flexibility). ■ Cost savings can be made because standardised machinery can be used. ■ The need for highly skilled workers is reduced, therefore reducing costs.	■ Resources (eg equipment and employees) may have nothing to do in between each batch, which is costly. ■ Employee motivation can be less than job production because they will carry out the same, often repetitive, task in each batch. ■ A fault or error in one item can lead to the whole batch being wasted. ■ The cost of each item could be high if only small batches are being made.

Flow production (line production)

This is when parts are added to the product being made as it moves along the production line. The final product will have been manufactured by the time it reaches the end of the production line. It is sometimes called line production. Examples: cars, computers, other electrical items.

Advantages of flow production	Disadvantages of flow production
■ Large quantities of identical products can be made. ■ Machinery is often used for the whole production process saving on labour costs (this is known as **automation**). ■ Raw materials can be purchased in bulk, meaning economies of scale can be taken advantage of. ■ Machinery can work 24 hours a day, 7 days a week. ■ Quality can be easily checked at various stages.	■ Products cannot be made to the customer's individual requirements. ■ Motivation can be low among employees due to the repetitive nature of the tasks they do. ■ A fault or breakdown in one part of the production line could cause production to stop which could be costly. ■ Mass demand for identical products needed.

Labour and capital intensive

The quantity of capital (machinery and equipment) or labour (humans) used in an organisation determines whether it is **labour** or **capital** intensive.

Automation means that machinery has replaced the need for employees to carry out the work required because machinery can do it instead.

Mechanisation involves machinery as well as some degree of labour in the production process. For example, people may still be required to operate some parts of the machinery being used.

	Advantages	Disadvantages
Labour intensive	■ Employees can use their initiative when required. ■ There is always a supply of labour available. ■ Cheaper than purchasing expensive equipment and machinery.	■ Costly to recruit, select and train employees. ■ Accuracy and quality of work can vary.
Capital intensive	■ Machinery can work 24 hours, 7 days per week. ■ Accuracy and quality of work standardised.	■ Cannot meet individual and specific customer requirements. ■ Breakdowns can be costly. ■ Employees become tired and bored of the repetitive tasks they carry out and therefore morale and motivation can be low.

Sample examination questions

1. Describe three methods of production. (3 marks)
2. Discuss and justify the use of the following methods of production: job and flow. (4 marks)

Quick Test 25

1. Identify the three methods of production.
2. Suggest the method of production that would be most suitable for mass producing an item.
3. Explain what is meant by the term mechanisation.
4. Will a capital intensive production process rely more heavily on machinery or people?

Managing Quality

What is quality?

This is a difficult question to answer. How can we put into words what quality is? It is perhaps easier to describe what high quality is and what poor quality is.

Customers expect products to be of a high quality. This means that the product works in the way it should, first time, with no problems, has been manufactured using high quality raw materials and its physical appearance looks good. The product should have been delivered on time and an after sales service should be provided.

Poor quality is the exact opposite of high quality. A poor quality product will not work the way it should, it may have been made with poor quality raw materials and its physical appearance is poor.

Organisations **must** ensure they produce high quality products. By doing so, it will meet the expectations of customers who in turn may make repeat purchases and encourage other people to purchase from that organisation. Remember, it is operating in a highly competitive environment and if customers are not satisfied with the product quality, they will go elsewhere. By providing a high quality product, the organisation will have the best chance of maximising profit and retaining, if not growing, its market share. It will have minimised wastage and therefore have kept costs low in this respect.

Organisations use a variety of strategies or methods to ensure quality as detailed below.

Top Tip

Questions on methods of ensuring and achieving quality have been **very** common in the final SQA examination in recent years. Study this section carefully!

Ensuring quality

Quality assurance	Quality assurance involves checking the product at various stages of the production process. It attempts to reduce wastage by knowing in advance what the standard expected should be and any product that does not meet the standard is disregarded.
Quality control	Quality control involves checking the product once it has been manufactured. Any product that does not meet the necessary standard will be scrapped.
Quality Management	Quality Management was previously referred to as Total Quality Management (TQM). Quality Management is **more than** just checking a product either during or after the production process. It involves the whole organisation where commitment to quality is second nature and where the aim is to produce the perfect product because no errors are acceptable. The customer's definition of quality is crucial. Quality Management requires: ■ Every person in the organisation to be involved in setting quality standards. ■ The aim and goal of constant improvement. ■ Team working and commitment at all levels of the hierarchy.

	<ul><li>The constant checking and monitoring of product standards and, where necessary, improvements made.</li><li>Ongoing and constant employee training.</li><li>The existence of policies where quality is clearly defined.</li></ul>
Benchmarking	Benchmarking involves comparing one product with another similar product, often using the market leader's standards as the benchmark. The organisation will attempt to match these standards.
Quality circles	Quality circles involve members of the organisation meeting regularly to discuss quality issues and then attempting to find ways to solve these. It will involve employees at all levels of the hierarchy and employee motivation can increase as they are being involved in the decision making process.

Organisations must ensure that all inputs into the production process are of the highest quality to ensure that the output is of the highest quality.

Between ensuring product quality and quality of other inputs such as raw materials and employee training.

Quality standards

Quality standards are awarded to an organisation when it meets a particular specification. Being awarded a quality standard (or symbol) has benefits to both the organisation and the customer.

The organisation benefits from:

- Having a recognised symbol attached to its name and therefore its name and image is improved
- Having proof that it has met specific quality standards
- Having a competitive advantage over similar products and organisations which do not have quality standards.

Examples of quality standards are:

BS5750 – This is the benchmark standard in the UK for quality.
ISO9000 – This is the international equivalent of the UK's BS5750.
Kite Mark – This shows a product has been made to the standards identified by the British Standards Institution (BSI).

Investors in People – This is a quality standard that can be given to organisations that provide training and development opportunities to its employees.

The role of other departments

Other departments in the organisation have a role to play in providing quality.

Human Resources

- Should recruit and select appropriately skilled and qualified individuals
- Should provide high quality training
- Have a system in place for recognising employees' strengths and areas for improvement (appraisal).

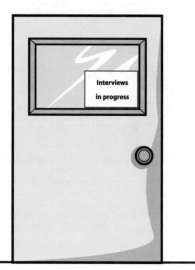

Marketing

- Should obtain feedback from customers (market research) and where necessary, act on this feedback.
- Testing and developing new products thoroughly can help identify any problem areas.

 Between other departments who have key roles in providing a quality good or service.

Sample examination questions

1. Explain measures organisations can take to ensure they produce a quality product or service. (9 marks).
2. Discuss the importance of quality inputs in the operations process of an organisation. (4 marks)
3. Describe how the introduction of Quality Management (formerly TQM) techniques could ensure a quality product or service is introduced. (5 marks)
4. Explain how the Human Resource Department can help to ensure that a quality product or service is produced. (4 marks)

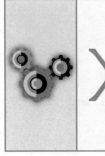

Purchasing mix	Operating system	Fixed rate	Piece rate
Flat rate	Fringe benefits	Quality standards	Quality circles
Quality assurance	Quality control	Quality Management	Inputs
Benchmarking	Job, batch, flow production	Capital intensive	Warehouse
Labour intensive	Automation	Mechanisation	Economic stock level
Decentralised storage	Centralised storage	Outputs	Distribution mix
EPOS	Stock management	Lead time	Just in time

Congratulations!

Congratulations on reaching the end of Unit 2: Business Decision Areas: Marketing and Operations! This is a good opportunity for you to review what you have learned during the unit, and ask your teacher/lecturer for help on anything you do not understand. Make sure you complete the section on 'Tracking Your Learning Journey'.

Quick Test 26

1. Explain the difference between quality control and quality assurance.
2. Describe what is meant by a quality circle.
3. Suggest a benefit to an organisation of having a quality standard.

Organisations and Finance

Important study note

Some people sometimes find parts of this topic difficult, but don't just ignore it if you are one of these people. You might be able to avoid answering some finance questions in your exam (depending on the optional questions you choose) but you can't ignore any compulsory exam question and you certainly cannot afford to ignore these questions in your Unit 3 NAB! (50% of the marks in your Unit 3 NAB are based on this topic.) **Please take your time to work through and revise any Finance topic you are unsure of.**

Role and importance of finance

Finance is a very important resource. It is needed to achieve objectives (eg survival, growth) and to carry out a number of activities. Organisations will usually have a Finance department whose role it is to manage the organisation's finance. There will be a number of different people employed in this department from accountants to wages assistants to credit controllers.

The role of the Finance department involves carrying out the following activities:

It is important it does these tasks for a number of reasons:

- Employees must be paid the correct amount. If their pay is wrong or late they may become unhappy and it could impact upon any personal items of expenditure they need to pay (eg mortgage and household bills).
- It must prepare financial statements, such as budgets, to help management in decision making. If the budget shows a deficit (more money going out than coming in) the organisation would need to act upon this.
- Bills and accounts must be paid on time to ensure the organisation maintains a good reputation and relationship with its suppliers and to enable it to maintain a good credit rating.

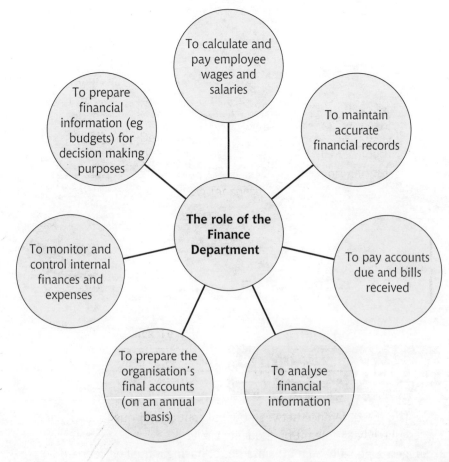

Uses of financial information

Financial information has considerable uses and we have already looked at some of these uses. Other uses include:

To enable costs and expenditure to be controlled

Costs and expenses must be controlled to avoid financial problems and the need to borrow money to cover these costs. Where necessary, management might have to take action to reduce costs and the amount of money going out of the organisation.

To enable cash flow going in and out of the organisation to be monitored

Money coming into the organisation and going out of the organisation (as above) needs to be monitored. Organisations need to have enough 'cash' available to be able to pay bills and employee wages. Making profit and having a good cash flow are two different things.

To forecast what might happen in the future

Preparing budgets and looking at past financial records can help management identify trends and to see what may happen in the future. Where necessary, action can be taken to avoid financial problems. Budgets can be prepared to forecast the organisation's future cash flow position.

To monitor the organisation's performance

Financial information from one year can be compared against previous years and against competitors. This is useful to see if action taken in the past has worked and, where necessary, to take action in the future. This may involve carrying out ratio analysis.

To provide management with information for decision making

We have already discovered that management make lots of decisions (see Chapter 4). Financial information plays a crucial role in the decision making process and will often decide which course of action is to be taken.

> Between uses of financial information and the impact on decision making.

Quick Test 27

1. Identify three activities carried out by the Finance department.
2. Suggest a reason why it is important that bills are paid on time.
3. Identify the financial statement that can be prepared to forecast the organisation's future cash flow position.
4. What % of marks is allocated to Finance in the Unit 3 NAB?
5. Are you able to miss out studying the Finance topic just because you might not like it? Or find some of it difficult?

Final Accounts

Organisations must prepare a set of final accounts every year (annually). These final accounts consist of two things: **Trading, Profit and Loss Account** and a **Balance Sheet**.

Final accounts are prepared for good reasons; they provide a summary of the transactions (revenue and costs) **that have taken place** over the **past** financial period, eg a year. They are used for many different reasons by various stakeholders (see page 16).

Top Tip

You will not be asked to prepare a set of Final Accounts in this course. However, you could be asked questions on the different parts of the Final Accounts and what they mean.

> Between the different types of business organisations and whether or not they have to publish their final accounts.

Trading, Profit & Loss Account

This shows a summary of the money that has came in (revenue) and gone out (costs) of the organisation over a particular period of time (usually one year). The **Trading Account** shows the **Gross Profit** whereas the **Profit and Loss Account** shows the **Net Profit**. The amount of tax the organisation has to pay is based upon the Net Profit figure.

Try copying out the Trading, Profit and Loss Account shown and changing some of the figures. Look at what happens to the Gross and Net Profit figure when things (eg amount of expenses or sales) change.

The amount of money made from **Sales** less **Cost of Sales.** Note – it will be a GROSS LOSS if the Cost of Sales is greater than the Sales figure.

Expenses are items the organisation needs to pay for.

This is the amount of money made (Profit) after expenses have been subtracted from the Gross Profit. It could be a NET LOSS.

Trading, Profit & Loss Account of Robin Electricals for year ending 31 December 20__

	£000	£000
Sales		300
Less Cost of Sales		
Opening Stock	40	
Add Purchases	150	
	190	
Less Closing Stock	20	
Cost of Goods Sold		170
GROSS PROFIT		**130**
Less Expenses:		
Rent	10	
Advertising	8	
Electricity	3	
Telephone	15	
Wages	10	46
NET PROFIT		**84**

The Balance Sheet

The **Balance Sheet** shows the value of the organisation at a particular point in time. It shows what the organisation owns **(assets)** and what debts **(liabilities)** it has.

These are items owned by the organisation that will last for longer than one year.

These are items owned by the organisation that will last for less than a year.

Liabilities are debts. Short-term liabilities are 'Current', eg creditors, and there are also 'Long-term' liabilities such as a bank loan.

This is simply Current Assets less Current Liabilities. There should be more Current Assets than Current Liabilities. Sometimes known as *Net Current Assets*.

The **Financed by** section towards the bottom of the Balance Sheet shows where the money for the organisation originally came from.

This is what the owner has withdrawn from the organisation throughout the year for their own use.

These are people who owe the organisation money because they will have bought goods on **credit**.

These are people who the organisation owes money to because the organisation bought goods on credit.

After subtracting liabilities, this shows the total value of the business.

The finance invested by the owner.

Balance Sheet of Robin Electricals as at 31 December __

	£000	£000
FIXED ASSETS		
Premises		250
Equipment		100
Vehicles		50
		400
CURRENT ASSETS		
Closing Stock	20	
Debtors	40	
Bank	50	
	110	
Less Current Liabilities		
Creditors	25	
Working Capital		85
Capital Employed		485
Financed by		
Opening Capital		420
Add Net Profit		84
		504
Less Drawings		19
		485

Quick Test 28

1. Identify the two types of business organisations that do not have to publish their accounts.
2. Explain the difference between Fixed Assets and Current Assets.
3. How is Working Capital calculated?
4. What will happen to the Net Profit figure if expenses were to increase?
5. What will happen to the Net Profit figure if expenses were to decrease?

Cash flow management

Cash is a crucial resource in any organisation. It is needed to pay bills, to purchase assets, to pay employees and to achieve different objectives. All organisations want to maximise profit, but they need cash on a day-to-day basis to operate. It is important that an organisation monitors its cash flow so that it can continue to operate successfully, meet its financial obligations and organise resources in the most efficient way. Many problems organisations face can be caused by a poor cash flow.

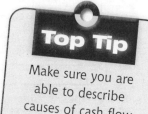

Failing to have a healthy cash flow can be caused by a number of reasons including:

- Having money tied up in stock
- Too much time given to customers to pay their debt (a long credit period)
- Not enough money being made from sales
- Too short a credit period being offered by creditors or suppliers
- The value of drawings taken out by owners has been high
- Spending money on capital items.

Cash flow problems can be solved in a number of ways. Some of the problems above could be solved by:

Top Tip

Make sure you are able to describe causes of cash flow problems and provide solutions to these problems that you can justify.

Suggestion	Justification
Introduce a 'Just in Time' approach to stock management	To save money being tied up in stock. By using a JIT system, stock is only purchased when it is needed for an order.
Offer discounts to customers to pay on time and preferably in cash	This will encourage customers to pay their bills more quickly and the cash received can be used to fund other activities and pay bills.
Increase advertising and promotion activities	Advertising can raise awareness of the organisation and its products. Different promotion activities (eg special offers) could be used to entice customers to buy. More being purchased increases sales and cash flow and reduces stock.
Sell assets that are no longer required	Selling assets which are no longer required will generate cash and because they are not required by the organisation it will not cause any disruption to the organisation's operations.

Organisations could also use additional sources of finance to manage their cash flow and these are discussed in more detail on page 90.

> Between different areas of the course (eg stock management and marketing) that can help solve cash flow problems.

Cash budget

To help manage cash and ensure control over future cash flow, organisations can prepare a **cash budget**. This is a **forecast** of the money they expect to receive (**receipts**) and the money they expect to pay out (**payments**) over a period of time in the future.

The benefits of preparing a cash budget include:

- Being able to identify when a negative cash balance **(a deficit)** may occur so that appropriate action can be taken (eg arranging additional finance)
- Being able to identify when a positive cash balance **(a surplus)** may occur as this could be used to finance other investments and make future decisions
- Being able to arrange additional sources of finance
- Previous budgets as well as forecasted ones can be used in decision making.

Top Tip

It would be a good idea to create a list of reasons why organisations prepare budgets. This type of question tends to be answered poorly!

A cash budget could be used as a target for the organisation and different departments within the organisation to work towards. In a large organisation each department may have its own budget and the authority for controlling (and spending!) this budget would be delegated to the department's manager. Management could compare the **actual** spending of the department with the amount budgeted to assess the department manager's skills in budgeting and ensuring that the money being spent is in line with the organisation's objectives. **(Remember – a budget is just a forecast into the future!)** It would be the responsibility of the department manager to ensure his/her department stays within budget and, where necessary, take action to ensure it does so. Similarly, the management of the organisation will be comparing the actual expenditure of the whole organisation against its budgeted expenditure and again taking action where necessary.

Here is what a cash budget looks like:

Cash Budget of Barry's Flying School for January and February		
	January	February
Opening Balance	1000	1800
Receipts		
Sales	5000	5500
Total Cash	6000	7300
Payments		
Purchases	2400	1900
Wages	1200	1600
Advertising	300	280
Rent	300	300
Insurance	450	450
Other Expenses		1250
Total Payments	4200	5780
Closing Balance	1800	1520

The Closing Balance of one month is the Opening Balance of the next.

Look at this example .... even though sales are going to be higher in February, the closing balance is going to be lower than January. This is because **payments** are likely to be higher in February.

Sample examination questions

1. Explain why managers use cash budgets. (5 marks)
2. Describe four causes of cash flow problems. (4 marks)
3. Profitable firms may fail due to poor cash flow. Identify four sources of cash flow problems and suggest one solution for each source you have identified. (8 marks)

Quick Test 29

1. Suggest a reason why it is important to have a healthy cash flow.
2. Suggest two reasons for having a poor cash flow.
3. What is a cash budget?
4. Explain the term deficit.

Using Financial Information

Users of financial information

We have already discussed how final accounts and cash budgets can be used to inform planning, decision making and resource organisation (eg stock), but we need to consider reasons why other stakeholders and not just the owners or managers of an organisation would be interested in financial information.

The final accounts can be used to show an organisation's **profitability, liquidity** and **efficiency**. This information is gathered by carrying out financial analysis using ratios. We will look at this on page 86.

- **Profitability** – *how profitable the organisation is*
- **Liquidity** – *how able the organisation is to pay its short-term debts*
- **Efficiency** – *shows if the organisation is performing effectively and efficiently.*

Some stakeholders, for example suppliers, will be more interested in how liquid the organisation is compared to how efficient it is.

Top Tip

Some users of financial information are internal (eg employees, managers) whereas some are external (eg government, suppliers).

Stakeholder	Interest in financial information
Employees	▪ To see whether or not the organisation is paying a fair wage (eg are they making large profits but not agreeing to pay raises?). ▪ To understand why certain decisions may be taken (eg redundancies, pay cuts). ▪ To assure themselves that the organisation is making profit and that their jobs are secure.
Inland Revenue (HMRC)	▪ To ensure the correct amount of taxation is being paid. This is based upon the Net Profit figure from the Trading, Profit & Loss Account.
Shareholders (Limited Companies)	▪ To make a decision on how to vote at the AGM. ▪ To decide whether to purchase additional shares. ▪ The current share price can be used to determine to sell or buy more shares ▪ To decide if the organisation is paying a fair dividend based on the profit made
Suppliers and other creditors	▪ Based on liquidity information a supplier or creditor may decide to give more credit ▪ Liquidity information will show how able the organisation is to pay off its short-term debts
Lenders (eg bank)	▪ To determine whether or not a loan or a bank overdraft should be issued. This would be based on all information available, but particularly profitability and liquidity. How liquid the organisation is would inform future loan payments.

In Chapter 1 we looked at the interest and influence of stakeholders.

Limitations of financial information

There is no doubt that decisions and management planning is based on a range of financial information but there are limitations to this. Not all decisions can be based purely on how profitable the organisation is or isn't! It must be remembered that the majority of financial information is based on past transactions and events.

When judging the success of an organisation, financial information (and the results of ratio analysis) cannot be used on its own to determine how successful it is because the following are not shown:

- The level of staff motivation or morale
- The impact of external factors on the organisation
- Future product developments or plans
- How successful the organisation has been in eliminating competition
- The product life cycle of the organisation's products
- Any changes in the organisation will not be reflected.

A competitor may decide to take over or merge with an organisation even if it isn't very profitable because:

- It has a range of valuable assets
- It has a strong brand name
- It has a large and loyal customer base.

Top Tip

Financial information does not reveal everything about an organisation. There are other factors that are important and need to be considered when judging how successful an organisation is.

Sample examination questions

1. Describe the problems that can occur when using only accounting information to analyse performance. (4 marks)
2. Describe how stakeholders could make use of financial information provided by an organisation. (7 marks)
3. Discuss the importance of the Annual Accounts in showing whether or not an organisation has achieved its objectives. (4 marks)

Quick Test 30

1. What does the term 'how liquid an organisation is' mean?
2. Suggest a reason why employees are interested in an organisation's financial information.
3. What can be calculated to aid financial analysis?
4. Suggest two reasons why an organisation may be taken over even if it isn't making a large profit.
5. For what reason might a bank be interested in an organisation's financial information?

Ratio Analysis

Important study note

As much as you might be tempted, **please do not** skip over this section. In this course you will not be asked to calculate ratios. However, you could be asked questions on the purpose and interpretation of ratios and it is for this reason that you should spend time learning them. You never know, you might enjoy it!!

What is ratio analysis?

Financial information can be analysed in more detail by carrying out ratio analysis. Ratio analysis can be used to compare an organisation's performance with past years and that of similar organisations. It can help identify trends and irregularities over a period of time. Where the results of ratio analysis give cause for concern, action can be taken to try to improve the ratio.

There are lots of ratios that can be used in financial analysis but for this course, we only need to consider six of them.

We can categorise different ratios depending on whether they provide information on **profitability, liquidity or efficiency**. For this course, however, the six ratios we study only belong to the profitability and liquidity categories.

Top Tip

Ask your teacher or lecturer for some exercises on calculating ratios. Compare the results from one year to the next and look at the reasons why the ratios may have changed. Also try comparing the ratios of similar organisations. If one has a better ratio than another, ask yourself why.

Profitability ratios

Profitability ratios measure how profitable the organisation is. They are used to analyse the organisation's expenses, cost of stock and the selling price.

Ratio	Interpretation	Why would it change?
Gross Profit Percentage **This ratio shows the profit made from the buying and selling of stock.** $\frac{\text{Gross Profit}}{\text{Sales}} \times 100 = \_\_\_\%$ The higher the % the better. If in Year 1 the ratio was 30% and in Year 2 it was 35% this shows that for every pound made from sales, more of it is gross profit in Year 2 than in Year 1.	If the ratio INCREASES this means more gross profit is being made from each pound of sales.	■ Selling price has been raised. ■ Cost of sales has been lower because cheaper suppliers have been used.
	If the ratio DECREASES this means less gross profit is being made from each pound of sales.	■ Cost of sales has increased. It would be necessary to find cheaper suppliers or negotiate discounts. ■ Stock has been lost due to theft or wastage. ■ Less marketing activities which has caused a decrease in sales. ■ Less sales have been made because a competitor has a better and more cost effective alternative.

Net Profit Percentage **This ratio shows the profit made once expenses have been made by the organisation.** $$\frac{\text{Net Profit}}{\text{Sales}} \times 100 = \underline{\quad}\%$$ The higher the % the better. If in Year 1 the ratio was 25% and in Year 2 it was 30% this shows that for every pound made from sales, more of it is net profit in Year 2 than in Year 1.	If the ratio INCREASES this means more net profit is being made from each pound of sales.	■ Gross profit has been higher. ■ Expenses have been lower because cheaper alternatives (eg for electricity supplies) have been sought.
	If the ratio DECREASES this means less net profit is being made from each pound of sales.	■ Gross profit has decreased (see reasons above). ■ Expenses have increased – it would be necessary to find cheaper alternatives.
Return on Capital Employed (ROCE) **This ratio shows the return on the capital investment made by the owner or shareholder in the organisation.** $$\frac{\text{Net Profit}}{\text{Capital Employed}} \times 100 = \underline{\quad}\%$$ The higher the % the better. If in Year 1 the ratio was 20% and in Year 2 it was 25%, this means in Year 2 you have made a return of 25%. For every £1 invested, you have made a return of 25p.	If the ratio INCREASES this means the owner or shareholder is making more of a return on their investment.	■ Sales have increased because of better marketing and therefore more profit has been made. ■ Expenses have been lower because a cheaper supplier is being used or because more discounts are being offered.
	If the ratio DECREASES this means the owner or shareholder is making less of a return on their investment.	■ Sales have decreased because of poor marketing and therefore less profit has been made. ■ Less sales have been made because a competitor has a better and more cost effective alternative. ■ Expenses have increased – it would be necessary to find cheaper alternatives.
Mark Up **This ratio shows how much profit has been added to the cost of goods sold.** $$\frac{\text{Gross Profit}}{\text{Cost of Goods Sold}} \times 100 = \underline{\quad}\%$$ The higher the % the better. If the ratio was 32% in Year 1 and 37% in Year 2, that more 'mark up' (or profit) has been added to product. If a product cost the organisation £1 and they sold it for £1·30 this would be a 30% mark up.	If the ratio INCREASES this means more profit has been made after the cost of goods.	■ Selling price has been raised. ■ Cost of sales has been lower because cheaper suppliers have been used.
	If the ratio DECREASES this means less profit has been made after the cost of goods sold.	■ Cost of sales has increased. It would be necessary to find cheaper suppliers or negotiate discounts. ■ Selling price has been lowered, perhaps to encourage more sales or to eliminate competition.

Liquidity ratios

Liquidity ratios show how able the organisation is to pay its short-term debts. They would indicate if an organisation needed to arrange additional finance to pay its bills.

Ratio	Interpretation	Why would it change?
Current Ratio *(also called the Working Capital Ratio)* **This ratio shows how able an organisation is to pay off its short-term debts.** $$\frac{\text{Current Assets}}{\text{Current Liabilities}} : 1$$ An ideal answer would be 2:1. This means it has doubled the value of current assets compared to current liabilities. If the answer was 1:1 or lower the organisation would struggle to pay its debts.	If the ratio INCREASES this means the organisation has an increased ability to pay off its short-term debts.	■ Current liabilities have decreased. ■ Current assets have increased.
	If the ratio DECREASES this means the organisation has less ability to pay off its short-term debts.	■ Current liabilities have increased. ■ Current assets have decreased.
Acid Test Ratio **This ratio shows how able an organisation is to pay off its short-term debts without having to sell its stock.** $$\frac{\text{Current Assets} - \text{Stock}}{\text{Current Liabilities}} : 1$$ A result of 1:1 is considered to be acceptable. If this was the case, it means the organisation could pay off its short-term debts without having to sell any stock.	If the ratio INCREASES this means the organisation has an increased ability to pay off its short-term debts.	■ Current liabilities have decreased. ■ Current assets have increased (but not the stock figure).
	If the ratio DECREASES this means the organisation has less ability to pay off its short-term debts.	■ Current liabilities have increased. ■ Current assets have decreased (but not the stock figure).

Efficiency ratios

Efficiency ratios show if the organisation is performing effectively and efficiently and how well the capital invested into the organisation is being utilised.

For this course, you do not need to know any efficiency ratios.

Problems using ratio analysis

There are problems or limitations of carrying out ratio analysis and using the results.

- The figures used to calculate the ratios are historic and do not show what could happen in the future.
- Comparisons between different organisations are difficult because the results are only valid when compared with an organisation of the same type and size.
- External factors are not taken into account.
- The results do not consider problems with human resources and the workforce (eg staff motivation or morale).
- Ratio analysis does not take into account any new product developments or launches.

 Between the impact of external factors on the organisation and its profitability, liquidity and efficiency.

Sample examination questions

1. Describe ratios which could be used to ensure that appropriate levels of profitability and liquidity are maintained. (5 marks)
2. Describe the limitations of using ratio analysis. (3 marks)
3. Describe the actions an organisation could take to improve the Net Profit Percentage and Current Ratios. (6 marks)

Quick Test 31

1. Suggest a reason why organisations use ratio analysis.
2. What do profitability ratios show?
3. Identify the formula used to calculate the ROCE ratio.
4. What difference is there between the current ratio and the acid test ratio?

Sources of finance

Source	Description	
Bank loan	A bank loan is a sum of money that is given to a business, which must be paid back at a later date. Normally, interest is charged on the loan.	
	Advantages	**Disadvantages**
	■ Regular payments are made that are of fixed amounts (therefore easier to budget). ■ Large sums of loans can be requested.	■ Interest is payable on the amount borrowed. ■ A bank loan may not be given if the bank has concerns about an organisation's financial position and its ability to pay it back.
Bank overdraft	An overdraft is when a bank agrees to a business taking more money out of their bank account than is available.	
	Advantages	**Disadvantages**
	■ Generally easy to arrange. ■ Interest is only charged on how much is borrowed and for the number of days the overdraft has been used.	■ Charges for having an overdraft can be expensive. ■ Usually only suitable for the short term.
Mortgage	A mortgage is like a loan that is given to buy, eg the premises for a business, but the key difference is that the mortgage is secured against the property being bought.	
	Advantages	**Disadvantages**
	■ Fixed interest rate mortgages can be arranged and the organisation would know exactly how much is to be paid back each month. ■ Can be taken out over a long period of time (eg often 25 years or longer).	■ Usually secured against the property being bought. If the organisation fails to keep up with repayments, the mortgage provider could repossess the property. ■ Mortgage providers are asking for larger deposits in today's economic climate.
Government grant	A grant is a sum of money given to an organisation which does not need to be paid back.	
	Advantages	**Disadvantages**
	■ Does not need to be repaid.	■ Usually only given once. ■ May not be a huge amount of money.
Share issues	Limited companies could issue extra shares. Plcs would issue these on the stock market.	
	Advantages	**Disadvantages**
	■ Large amounts of capital can be obtained. ■ Shareholders benefit from limited liability. ■ Finance raised does not need to be paid back in the way loans do.	■ Share selling prices vary. ■ It could be expensive to issue more shares. ■ Organisations are only authorised to issue a certain number of shares.
Leasing	Leasing means to rent. Businesses could rent equipment, for example, rather than having to raise the finance to buy these outright.	
	Advantages	**Disadvantages**
	■ Saves on having to purchase expensive equipments outright. ■ Equipment can be changed and kept up-to-date.	■ Could prove expensive to lease over a long period of time. ■ The equipment is not owned by the organisation so therefore is not an asset to them.

➡

Hire purchase	An item is purchased which remains the property of the seller until all payments have been made. The buyer usually needs to provide an initial deposit and then pay the remaining balance of equal instalments over a period of time.	
	Advantages	**Disadvantages**
	■ The item is owned by the organisation once all payments have been made. ■ Saves on having to spend large sums of money at one time.	■ Interest charged can be very expensive. ■ If the organisation fails to meet payments, the hire purchase company can repossess the item purchased.
Trade credit	Items are purchased but paid for at a later date. The seller of the items is a creditor to the buyer until items have been paid for.	
	Advantages	**Disadvantages**
	■ Can be used to help an organisation when cash flow is poor.	■ Cash discount for paying quickly is not given. ■ Any payments missed may damage the relationship between the buyer and seller, which could result in future trade credit being refused.
Venture capitalists (Business Angels)	Venture capitalists (sometimes known as 'Business Angels') provide large loans to those organisations which a bank or other lender may assess as being too much of a risk. They usually part-own the organisation in return.	
	Advantages	**Disadvantages**
	■ Organisations whose credit rating is poor or who are deemed to be of a high risk to lend to can get finance from venture capitalists. ■ Large loans can be obtained.	■ Not suitable in the short term or for loans of small amounts. ■ Can be expensive. ■ Part-ownership of the organisation may be requested in exchange for the finance they are willing to provide.

 Between different types of organisations and the sources of finance that are suitable for them.

Sample examination questions

1. Describe and justify three sources of finance that could be used to expand a business. (6 marks)
2. Other than a grant, describe three sources of finance available to a public limited company trying to solve the problem of a lack of development finance. (3 marks)

Trade credit	Hire purchase	Profitability	Balance sheet
Wage/Salary	Cash budget	Creditor	Fixed assets
Venture capitalist	Ratio analysis	Efficiency	Capital
Current liabilities	Liquidity	Trading Account	Leasing
Debtor	Trade credit	Profit & Loss Account	Mortgage
Working capital	Deficit	Surplus	Bank Loan

Quick Test 32

1. Identify two sources of short-term finance.
2. Describe what is meant by hire purchasing.
3. Identify the source of finance that is often used when an organisation is considered to be risky.
4. Identify the source of finance that is only available to limited companies.

Human Resources and Changing Employment Patterns

What is Human Resource Management?

The role of the Human Resource Management function is important and plays a key role in enabling the organisation to meet its objectives. An organisation's employees are its greatest asset because they drive the organisation forward and are actively involved in implementing procedures, targets and goals. The organisation must recruit and develop their workforce in line with their HR policies, the law and their overall objectives.

The role of the HRM function can be remembered more easily by remembering the word **FACES**.

F	**Facilitator role**	The provision and delivery of management training and guidance will be done by the HRM department.
A	**Auditor role**	HRM policies and procedures must be followed by all those in the organisation and the HRM department will monitor and report on this.
C	**Consultancy role**	Specialist information and guidance will be given by the HRM department to managers on handling different matters and particular situations.
E	**Executive role**	The HRM department are experts on employment and HR matters.
S	**Service role**	The HRM department must ensure that all employees and management are kept up-to-date with changes in HR information, procedures and law.

Top Tip

In a question on the role of HR, you should be referring to FACES in your answer. It is not enough at Higher level to simply say 'HR deals with staff issues'.

In carrying out their various roles, staff in the HRM department will carry out a number of different activities:

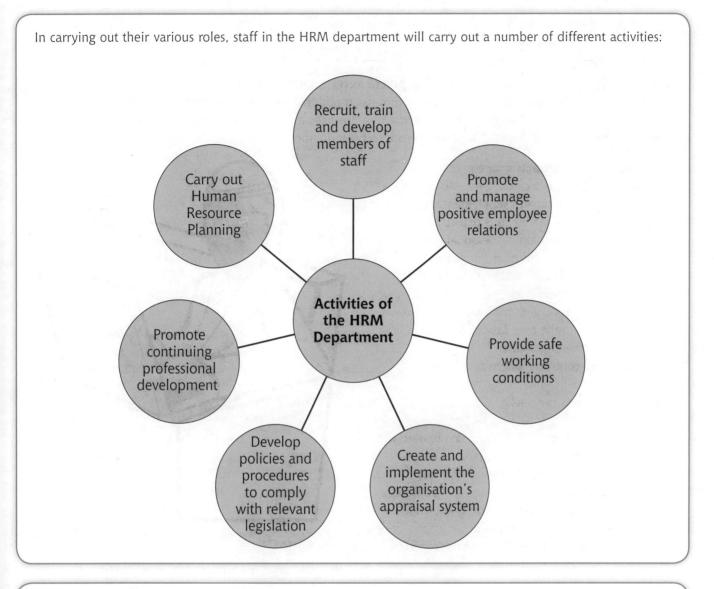

Changing employment patterns

There has been a considerable change in employment patterns in the UK over the last twenty or so years.

- There has been an increase in employment opportunities in the tertiary sector and a decrease in the primary/secondary sectors because of deindustrialisation.
- More people are being employed on **part-time** and **temporary** contracts compared to **full-time** or **permanent** ones.
- More women are now in employment in both full-time and part-time jobs and there has also been an increase in the number of women in management positions.
- Developments in ICT have allowed more people to work out of the office either as **homeworkers** or **teleworkers**.
- People have recognised the advantages of becoming self-employed and are opting to do this.
- As a result of the increase in the self-employed there are now many more smaller businesses in existence.

Human Resource planning is essential in keeping up with changing patterns of employment and in meeting an organisation's objectives. Human Resource planning involves monitoring changes and trends in the labour market to establish changes in employment patterns. It is essential to be able to identify and estimate which employees will be required in the future and whether changes to existing staff levels, contracts and working practices need to be made. HR planning also involves considering the skills that will be required to carry out future job roles and developing the appropriate training programmes to meet these requirements.

Working practices

We have come across the concept of **working practices** on a number of occasions now, but what does it actually mean? There has been a shift away from the traditional Monday to Friday 9am–5pm and organisations have had to develop a range of working practices to achieve their objectives and to keep up with changing employment patterns. They have introduced working practices such as:

- **Temporary contracts** where people are employed on a casual basis and only for a short period of time to supplement the core number of staff. This is particularly common when an organisation has seasonal fluctuations to cope with. At Christmas, for example, many organisations including the Post Office and large retailers employ people on temporary contracts to cope with the increase in demand, in addition to the **core labour force** who are crucial to the organisation.
- **Part-time contracts where** people work less hours than a full-time person and usually only a couple of days per week.
- Allowing people to work from home **(homeworking)** using ICT to communicate with the organisation when necessary.
- Allowing people to work away from the office and communicate with the organisation when necessary using ICT. This is known as **teleworking** and a good example is sales people who work away from the office but regularly communicate with the organisation using a range of ICT such as e-mail, laptops and Personal Digital Assistants.

There are benefits to both the employee and the organisation of having flexible working practices.

Benefits for the employee	Benefits for the organisation
■ People can balance their personal and work commitments more easily and therefore have a better work/life balance. ■ Own start and finishing times can often be chosen. ■ Travelling time and cost can be reduced. ■ Less stressful as they are more in control of their work and personal commitments.	■ Staff are generally more motivated and are therefore more productive. ■ There will be a reduced number of absences and incidents of late coming. ■ Space and money can be saved in the office if employees are working out of the office. ■ Potential employees may be attracted to an organisation who can offer flexible working practises so an organisation can recruit higher quality staff more easily

> Between different types of ICT and how they can be used by home and teleworkers.

Sample examination questions

1. Describe the changing patterns of employment that have occurred in the UK during the past twenty years.
2. Discuss the effects on an organisation of employing staff on temporary contracts. (4 marks)

Quick Test 33

1. Identify three roles carried out by the HRM department.
2. Identify two activities carried out by the HRM department.
3. Explain why Human Resource planning is important.
4. Describe what is meant by a temporary contract.

Recruitment

Stages in recruitment

Organisations carry out **recruitment** which means encouraging people to apply for a job vacancy. It is important that the highest quality of people are attracted to the organisation because they are a key ingredient in providing a quality output and achieving an organisation's objectives. It is important to spend time (and money!) on recruitment so that the organisation benefits from recruiting the highest quality employees in the long run.

Recruitment involves various stages:

Identifying a Job Vacancy

It may seem obvious but first the organisation needs to identify that a job actually exists. It may be that someone needs to be replaced or because an increase in demand has caused an increased workload that needs to be addressed.

Carrying out a Job Analysis

The next stage is to carry out a job analysis to see whether or not a job actually exists. This involves looking carefully at the vacancy and deciding which tasks would be carried out, what the responsibilities of the employee would be and what skills are needed to be able to carry out the job.

Preparing a Job Description

Having carried out the job analysis, a detailed document of what the job entails can be drawn up. This is known as the job description and contains information on: the job title, job purpose, tasks and responsibilities. It would also provide information on the pay, working hours, number of day's holiday entitlement and any benefits attached to the job (eg company car). The location of where the employee would be based is also given.

Preparing a Person Specification

Having carried out a job analysis and prepared a job description, the organisation can now decide what type of person would be most suitable for the job vacancy. The person specification provides this information. Certain skills, qualifications, personal attributes and experiences may be required to fulfil the requirements of the job, and the person specification contains this information. The person specification can be used as a tool in the selection process as it provides a list of what is essential and what is desirable for a candidate to have. The organisation can use this to assess each applicant's suitability for the vacancy.

Advertising the Job Vacancy

The organisation needs to make people aware that a job vacancy exists and they do this by advertising it. A job can be advertised in various places **internally** (eg staff notice board or though e-mail) and **externally** (eg in a newspaper, job centre website or at a college/university).

Top Tip

Recruitment is not the same as selection. Selection involves using different methods to choose the best candidate from those who have applied for a job.

Top Tip

When asked to describe the stages of the recruitment process, it is not enough at Higher level to simply list the stages involved, eg identify a job vacancy or carry out a job analysis. A detailed description of what happens at that stage is required. You should aim to write at least a couple of points for each stage in your answer.

Internal and external recruitment

Job vacancies can be advertised internally or externally and therefore are available to either **internal candidates only** or to **internal and external candidates**. There are advantages and disadvantages to both types of recruitment and you need to know them!

Internal recruitment	The job vacancy is only advertised within the organisation and therefore only those people already working for the organisation can apply for it.	
	Advantages	**Disadvantages**
	<ul><li>Existing employees are known by the organisation and if chosen will have been so because they have demonstrated they have the ability to do the job.</li><li>Employees feel more valued and can become more motivated and productive if given the chance of promotion.</li><li>Money can be saved on advertising, recruiting, selecting and training.</li><li>Existing employees are already familiar with the organisation's policies, procedures and organisation culture. There is therefore no need in this respect to spend time or money on training.</li></ul>	<ul><li>The opportunity to bring a person with a fresh outlook or new ideas into the organisation is lost.</li><li>There may not be an existing employee who has the skills or qualities to carry out the job.</li></ul>
External recruitment	The job vacancy is advertised both within and outwith the organisation and therefore anyone (whether an existing employee or not) can apply.	
	Advantages	**Disadvantages**
	<ul><li>People with new ideas can be brought into the organisation.</li><li>Can attract large quantities of applicants.</li></ul>	<ul><li>Existing employees who apply but do not get the job may feel unvalued and therefore lose the motivation to work hard.</li><li>It can be expensive to advertise in a range of external places. For example, the cost of advertising a vacancy in a national newspaper is expensive.</li><li>No matter how good the selection methods are, because the person is unknown, there is a chance that the wrong person could be chosen.</li></ul>

Sample examination questions

1. Describe the recruitment process that may be used by a Human Resource department. (5 marks)
2. Describe and explain the purpose of the following when recruiting new staff. (6 marks)
   i) Job description   ii) Person specification   iii) Reference

Quick Test 34

1. Describe what is meant by 'recruitment'.
2. Identify the recruitment stage that comes before preparing a job description.
3. How many points in a question on the stages of the recruitment process should you write in your answer for <u>each</u> stage?
4. Identify two places where a job vacancy could be advertised internally.
5. Describe an advantage of external recruitment.

Selection

Stages in selection

Having advertised the job and encouraged people to apply, the organisation now needs to decide how to choose the best person for the job; this is the role of selection. Organisations can use one or more methods of selection to choose the right person. However, the more methods used the greater the chance of selecting the best person for the job and eliminating those who are not suitable. The different selection methods that an organisation can use all have the aim of assessing the applicants' suitability against the essential and desirable skills, attributes and qualities contained in the person specification.

Short listing

Usually the first stage in the selection process is for people to submit an **application form** and/or **Curriculum Vitae** (CV) together with **references**. There can be hundreds of people applying for one job and it would be impossible and expensive to consider all of these further by interviewing or using another selection method. Instead, the organisation can read through each individual applicant's application form or CV and references and decide who to take to the next stage of the selection process. This is known as **short listing** or **leeting.**

Application forms	Application forms are designed and issued by the organisation on receipt of a request for them. They ask specific pieces of information that the organisation has requested to know. The applicant then fills it in.
Curriculum Vitae	CVs are designed by the applicant and only the information that the applicant wishes to disclose would be contained within it. However, CVs have the advantage of letting the applicant disclose and present information about them in a way they choose.
References	A reference is a report on a person by another individual or organisation. Often previous employers or training providers will provide references. They can back up the information contained within an application form or CV as well as providing key comments on the applicant's personality, attitude at work and suitability for the job applied for. It is not uncommon for at least two references to be requested and normally friends or family of the applicant would not be able to provide a reference.

After short listing

Once the short list has been created, the organisation now needs to assess each applicant on the short list further. This can be done by using a variety of selection methods including interviews, tests and assessment centres. Every organisation varies in which selection methods it uses, but for this course you need to be aware of all the different selection methods given below.

Interviews

Interviews are common in the selection process. They can take the format of **one-to-one, successive** or **panel interviews**.

One-to-one interviews	One interviewer interviews all of the short listed applicants and then makes a decision on who to select. This type of interview is not uncommon, but has a distinct disadvantage in that the interviewer may not like a particular applicant for whatever reason (eg personality) and this could lead to the wrong person being chosen.
Successive interviews	In this case there are several interviewers who interview each candidate separately. Unfortunately, it will mean for the applicant that they have a number of interviews to attend! It does however have the advantage over one-to-one interviews in that the problem of one interviewer disliking or favouring a particular applicant does not arise.
Panel interviews	A panel interview is when an applicant is interviewed by several people at one time. Each person on the interview panel asks a number of questions and each member has a final say in who is selected.

Top Tip

Remember, interviews are not the only selection method. The more selection methods used the greater chance of selecting the correct person for the job.

Testing

A variety of tests can be carried out to help in the selection process. Each test will assess a different aspect of the applicant and can provide useful information as well as confirming (or not!) the information given on the application form, CV or at interview. However, they are expensive for the organisation to carry out both financially and because they are time consuming. Testing needs to be carried out with caution because, just like exams, people can perform worse than expected because of the stress imposed on them. *(But because you will be extremely prepared for your Business Management exam, this won't happen to you.)*

Psychometric tests	In these tests, applicants are asked questions which will assess their personality. They can be used to find out what type of person they are and whether they suit the requirements of the job. Unlike some other tests, there is no correct answer and applicants should give truthful answers so that an accurate picture of their personality can be built up. However, they do not always give the truthful answer but the one they think an organisation would want to hear.
Aptitude tests	This test assesses the natural abilities of applicants on the skills required for the job they are applying for. Examples of aptitude tests include ones to assess literacy and numeracy skills.
Intelligence tests	Also known as IQ tests, these assess the mental capability of the applicant. Questions in these tests centre on problem solving and thinking skills, numeracy and literacy. Each applicant is given a score at the end of the test which can be compared to other applicants.
Medical tests	A doctor or nurse examines each applicant for any medical issues or concerns that may impact upon their ability to perform the duties of the job. Some occupations (eg emergency services and the army) have strict medical conditions to be met.
Attainment tests	An attainment test allows the organisation to test the applicant demonstrating specific skills. A requirement of an Administrative Assistant's job could be that they must be able to type 30 words per minute. An attainment test could prove whether they can or cannot.

Assessment centres

Assessment centres allow an organisation to see applicants undertaking a variety of tasks in different situations and scenarios and can sometimes take place over a couple of days. Many large organisations have assessment centres where they get applicants to take part in role play exercises, team building activities and make presentations. Applicants may have to undertake tests during the assessment centre. At all points during the assessment centre, the organisation will be watching each applicant carefully and making a note of their communication, team work and problem solving skills. Assessment centres are common in the aviation industry and airlines recruiting, for example cabin crew, will often carry out an assessment centre to help them in the selection process.

What happens next?

Once the organisation has carried out the selection methods it has chosen to use, it now needs to decide who to employ. This decision will be based upon all the information available, and sometimes one selection method may have more importance than another.

The successful applicant will be offered the position and those unsuccessful will be informed. It is good practice upon request from the unsuccessful applicant, for the organisation to offer feedback on their performance.

Sample examination questions

1. Explain the role of testing in the selection of new staff. (4 marks)
2. Discuss the different types of testing that an organisation could use to select the best candidate. (6 marks)

Quick Test 35

1. Describe what is meant by a reference.
2. Identify three types of testing.
3. Explain the difference between an application form and a CV.
4. Explain what is meant by short listing.

Training and Development

Employee training and development is essential in ensuring employees work as efficiently as possibly and in ensuring the organisation achieves its objective of providing a high quality good or service. New employees require training to introduce them to the demands and requirements of their new role.

Organisations who provide quality training and who encourage employees to develop themselves can gain a good image and reputation because they are seen to be promoting continuous professional development and life long learning. In today's business environment this is essential and is something both the UK and Scottish Governments are keen to promote.

Top Tip

Providing opportunities for employees to develop is important. It lies at the heart of the organisation achieving success and its aims.

Types of training

Induction training	Induction training provides new employees with an introduction to the organisation, its policies and procedures. It usually takes place as soon as the employee begins his or her new job. Induction training will provide the new employee with: ■ Information about the organisation: its structure, objectives, working practices and procedures ■ Information about their job role and responsibilities ■ Information about where they will be working: such as where the fire exits are and what the arrangements are for breaks/lunch. Induction training aims to settle new employees into their new working environment in the hope that they begin contributing to the productivity and success of the organisation as soon as possible. It allows for any matters (eg policies and health and safety procedures) to be dealt with quickly.
On-the-job training	This is when training is provided within the organisation. The employee may be given appropriate training by their manager or another colleague in their own workplace and use the equipment they are already familiar with. On-the-job training is less expensive than off-the-job training and the training programme will have been designed specifically for the organisation and job in mind.
Off-the-job training	This is when training is provided out with the organisation by another organisation. The employee is taken out of their normal working environment to be trained in another location by specialist trainers. It could take place at a college or university.

Costs and benefits of training

There are costs and benefits of training to both the organisation and employee.

Benefits	Costs
■ Employees can become more highly motivated. ■ Employee may become more productive. ■ Quantity of wastage and products scrapped is lowered. ■ The quality of the work the employee is carrying out will improve.	■ Can be expensive. ■ Working time is lost when employees are being trained and therefore productivity may fail. ■ Some employees may be reluctant to receive training.

- It contributes towards giving the organisation a good name.
- Change can be introduced more easily.
- A range of skills can be developed among the workforce that can be used now or in the future.

- Additional employees may need to be used to cover for those employees who are away being trained, which costs money.
- Once employees have been trained they may find a more highly paid job with another organisation.

Methods of training

There are different **methods** of training that could be used regardless of the type of training they are undertaking. Training methods include coaching, presentations, job rotation, demonstrations and role plays.

Appraisals

An appraisal system aims to ensure employees are working to the best possible standard with the goal of achieving the organisation's aims. An appraisal system allows employees' strengths and development needs to be identified. Normally employees would meet with their line manager on a yearly basis and would have a formal meeting to discuss:

- What is going well?
- What could be done better?
- What is not going so well?
- What action could be taken to improve?

A written record of the appraisal meeting will be kept and where an employee has development needs, the employee would normally be given the opportunity to undertake appropriate training to improve.

Benefits of an appraisal system	Costs of an appraisal system
<ul><li>Those who have the potential to be promoted can be identified.</li><li>The employee receives feedback from their line manager.</li><li>Employees can become motivated if the appraisal has been positive.</li><li>Opportunities for the employee to develop their skills and performance are identified.</li></ul>	<ul><li>Employees can become demotivated if the appraisal has not been positive.</li><li>It is time consuming for the organisation to carry out.</li><li>Too many development needs could be identified which results in stress for the employee as a result and an increase in workload.</li></ul>

An informal appraisal system can also exist whereby no formal structure is followed. It could simply take the form of a chat whereby the employee receives praise for doing a task well or is given feedback on how to improve their performance next time.

Top Tip

An appraisal is a two-way process. The employee will receive feedback on their performance from their line manager but the employee would also be expected to think about and evaluate their own performance.

Top Tip

Appraisals can be motivating and demotivating for an employee depending on whether it is a positive or negative experience.

Sample examination questions

1. Describe the different forms of training that an organisation could use. (6 marks)
2. Describe the costs of staff training. (4 marks)
3. Discuss the value of an appraisal system. (4 marks)

Quick Test 36

1. Identify the type of training given when an employee starts a new job.
2. Explain the difference between on-the-job and off-the-job training.
3. Identify two methods of training.
4. What does an appraisal system aim to do?

Employee Relations

Having motivated and happy employees is a key ingredient to success in any organisation. Employees lie at the heart of the organisation and are fundamental to it achieving its objectives. Employees can be motivated by:

- Being able to take advantage of flexible working practices
- Being given financial and non-financial incentives to work hard and achieve targets
- Being given praise and constructive feedback on their performance
- Being given opportunities to use their own initiative and take responsibility for their own work.

Unfortunately, the relationship between employee and employer can break down for a number of reasons. This can result in reduced productivity, a decrease in motivation, breakdowns in communication and less chance of the organisation's objectives being achieved. These are the effects of poor employee relations.

Good employee relations

Good employer and employee relationships can be formed in a number of ways. Simply having a process for enabling employees to express their views on matters is one way, but there are others:

Trade unions	Trade unions have the role of representing employees on various employment-related matters. These include pay, working conditions, dismissal and any other work-related issue. Employees wishing to become a member of a trade union can do so and usually have to pay a fee. Trade unions act on behalf of their members and have a much larger voice, more experience and are better able to negotiate than individual employees on their own. This is known as **collective bargaining**.
Works councils	Representatives from among the organisation's employees are chosen to form a works council. The works council has the ability to access various types of information that relate to the organisation and has the authority to take part in decision making with the management of the organisation in matters that impact upon the workforce.

Quality circles (as discussed in Chapter 7 – Operations) are another method of ensuring good employee relations.

 Remember, other groups (eg pressure groups) and stakeholders can influence an organisation.

Industrial action

Employees who are unhappy with their working conditions or terms of employment, and where unsuccessful discussions have not reached an agreement, have the option of undertaking **industrial action**. This would only be classed as 'official' when a trade union has agreed that this should take place.

Industrial action can have serious negative consequences on an organisation such as:

- Production could come to halt
- Customers could be lost
- Their image and reputation could be damaged.

It is important to remember that industrial action does not always resolve the dispute between both parties. Sometimes the employer will simply threaten to make employees **redundant** if they refuse to accept the terms or conditions given to them.

Forms of Industrial Action
- **Boycott** – Refusal to carry out a new duty or use a new piece of equipment.
- **Go slow** – Employees deliberately work slower than normal.
- **Sit in** – Employees refuse to work and simply sit in the workplace.
- **Strike** – A refusal to enter the workplace. (Employees may form a 'picket line'.)
- **Overtime ban** – A refusal to work any extra time over the normal working hours.
- **Work to rule** – Only activities written in the contract of employment will be carried out.

Redundancy is when an employee or a number of employees are paid off because their job is no longer required or no longer exists. It can happen when the organisation can no longer afford to pay the number of employees it has or when demand for a good or service has decreased, resulting in less work for the organisation to carry out. Organisations have a strict procedure to follow by law when making staff redundant and must make a redundancy payment to those being laid off.

Staff that are not made redundant will worry about the safety of their own jobs and the quality of their work can decrease. They may be required to undertake additional tasks or duties as a result of less people working for the organisation, which in turn can increase their own workload and may require them to be re-trained in carrying out new tasks.

Grievances

A **grievance** is when an employee has a complaint to make regarding a work-related issue to their employer. They may be unhappy about something they have been asked to do or because of the way they feel they are being treated. Organisations will have in place a **grievance procedure** that will identify the steps an employee must follow when raising a grievance. As a last resort, an employee can take their grievance to an organisation who deals with employment-related matters (eg **ACAS**) or an **industrial tribunal**.

ACAS stands for the Advisory, Conciliation and Arbitration Service. It is an organisation that specialises in stopping and resolving disputes between employees and their employer.

Top Tip

Look at the ACAS website (www.acas.org.uk) for more information.

Sample examination questions

1. Describe types of industrial action that employees could take. (4 marks)
2. Explain the possible effects prolonged industrial action could have on an organisation. (5 marks)
3. Describe the role of each of the following in supporting employees and employers when disputes occur in the workplace: (i) Trade unions (ii) ACAS. (6 marks)

Quick Test 37

1. Why are good employee relations important?
2. Describe what is meant by a trade union.
3. Identify two forms of industrial action.
4. Describe what is meant by a grievance.

Law and the workplace

We have already discussed some of the pieces of legislation impacting upon an organisation. These include the Data Protection Act, Computer Misuse Act and Freedom of Information Act.

We now need to look at the pieces of legislation concerned with protecting the welfare and safety of employees.

We can group the various pieces of employment legislation into three categories:

- Employment issues
- Health and safety
- Equal opportunities

Top Tip

Individuals and organisations can be prosecuted for breaking the law and there can be very serious consequences.

Employment law

Equal Pay Act 1970

This law aims to ensure both men and women are paid the same for doing a job which is considered of the same value.

Employment Rights Act 1996

The legal rights and duties of both employer and employee are stated in this law. It states that:

- Within two months of starting a job, an employee has the right to be given a written contract of employment.
- Employees should be given a payslip that details how their pay has been calculated.
- Employees have specific rights concerning the termination of their employment and when taking maternity leave (details of which are given in the Act).

National Minimum Wage Regulations 1999

These regulations set out the minimum hourly rate that must be paid to employees. The rate payable depends on the age of the employee as follows: 16–17 year olds, 18–21 year olds and 22 years old or over.

Health and Safety law

Offices, Shops and Railways Premises Act 1963

This law provides a list of the minimum basic health and safety requirements employers must meet. It provides information on the requirements of toilet facilities, first aid facilities, cleanliness and workplace temperature.

Health and Safety at Work Act 1974

This law states the responsibilities of both the employee and employer in ensuring health and safety. It states that both have a responsibility to ensure health and safety. Employees must consider the health and safety of other people and not just themselves.

Top Tip

You should keep up-to-date with changes in the law and new Acts.

Equal Opportunity law

Sex Discrimination Act 1975

This law aims to prevent the discrimination of people on the basis of their gender or marital status. It would be illegal, for example, for an organisation to provide different conditions of service to a woman compared to a man. ➔

Race Relations Act 1976
This law aims to prevent the discrimination of people on the basis of their race, colour, religion or ethnic origin.

Disability Discrimination Act 1995
This law aims to prevent discrimination of people on the basis of a disability. Where necessary, organisations must make reasonable changes to allow those with a disability to access the workplace.

Employment Equality (Sexual Orientation) Regulations 2003
These regulations prevent the discrimination of people on the basis of their sexuality.

Equality Act 2010
This new Act aims to simplify and update existing equality legislation. Nine existing pieces of equality legislation now come under this one Act. This Act has consequences for all organisations and activities. Do some research to find out the main principles of this Act and how it may impact upon an organisation.

Top Tip

Check out the About Equal Opportunities website (www. aboutequal opportunities.co.uk) for more information on equal opportunities law.

Sample examination questions

1. Explain how the following legislation could impact upon an organisation. (6 marks)
   - Freedom of Information Act 2000
   - National Minimum Wage Regulations 1999
   - Employment Rights Act 1996
2. Employment legislation exists to protect workers. Describe the purpose of the: (3 marks)
   - Health and Safety at Work Act 1974
   - Race Relations Act 1976
   - Equal Pay Act 1970

Selection	Training	Grievance	Equality
FACES	Discrimination	Collective bargaining	Testing
Industrial action	ACAS	Recruitment	Selection
Appraisals	Works council	Redundancy	Trade union
Equal opportunities	Working practices	Core labour force	Assessment centre

Congratulations!

Congratulations on reaching the end of Unit 3: Business Decision Areas: Finance and Human Resource Management! This is a good opportunity for you to review what you have learned during the unit, and ask your teacher/lecturer for help on anything you do not understand. Make sure you complete the section on 'Tracking Your Learning Journey'.

Answers to Quick Tests

Quick Test 1

1. An entrepreneur is someone who comes up with a business idea and develops it. In doing so, they take risks, make decisions and use their initiative.
2. Land is all natural resources, labour is the human effort, capital is the equipment, machinery and money used by a business and enterprise is combining all of the factors of production.
3. Needs are essential for survival and wants are demanded after needs have been met.
4. Primary – extracting raw materials; secondary – manufacturing of products; tertiary – providing a service.

Quick Test 2

1. To make a profit.
2. To provide a service.
3. Limited companies benefit from limited liability.
4. Owned by the taxpayer and managed by government.
5. A company that operates in more than one country.

Quick Test 3

1. Targets for an organisation to work towards.
2. No
3. To maximise profit. This means to make as much profit as possible by maximising sales and keeping cost of sales low.
4. That the objective was long term
5. Describe.

Quick Test 4

1. Any person, group or organisation interested in an organisation's success.
2. Employees, management, suppliers, banks/lenders, government, local community, charity donors, taxpayers, customers, press/media.
3. Interest refers to why that stakeholder is concerned with the success of the organisation.
4. Influence refers to how much power that stakeholder has over the organisation.

Quick Test 5

1. Bank loan, bank overdraft, mortgage, government grant, leasing, retained profits.

2. A bank loan is a sum of money that is given to a business that must be paid back, with interest, at a later date.
3. Local authorities, Careers Scotland, Business Gateway, Inland Revenue, banks, local enterprise agencies, Prince's Trust.
4. Advice on starting, preparing business plans, payroll and taxation, how and where to obtain financial support.

Quick Test 6

1. To increase profit, to increase market share, to obtain economies of scale, to reduce risk and to raise the company's profile and brand.
2. Merger is when two companies of roughly equal size join together and a takeover is when one larger company takes over a small one.
3. Backward vertical integration occurs when a business takes over a supplier and forward vertical integration occurs when a business takes over a customer.
4. When one business splits into two separate organisations.

Quick Test 7

1. To reduce the risk of failure.
2. Political, Economic, Social, Technological, Environmental, Competition.
3. Introduction of new laws and impact of current law, government policies, provision of infrastructure, taxation rates.
4. Interest rates, inflation levels, exchange rates, changes in demand and levels of unemployment.
5. Increase.

Quick Test 8

1. Survey/questionnaire, observation, interview.
2. Internet websites, textbooks, newspapers and magazines.
3. Primary information has been gathered by the organisation itself whereas secondary information has not.
4. Internal information is gathered from the organisation's own records whereas external information is obtained from outwith the organisation.
5. Qualitative information is in the form of views or opinions whereas quantitative information is factual and can be counted or measured.

6. Letters, memos, reports, magazines, newsletters, internet websites.
7. Discussions, meetings, presentations, interviews, telephone calls.

Quick Test 9

1. Planning, monitoring and control, decision making, measuring performance, identifying new business opportunities.
2. This involves using financial information to see how well the business is doing.
3. Information not of value could result in a wrong decision being made.
4. Accurate, timely, complete, appropriate, available, cost effective, objective, concise.
5. The information is correct and contains no errors.

Quick Test 10

1. To assist in decision making, to collect and distribute information, to communicate with different people, to maintain records and to assist in the product design and manufacturing process.
2. Meetings can take place without people being in the same location through a computer link.
3. Computer Aided Manufacture.
4. Database software.
5. Spreadsheets can create 'what-if' situations which allow a business to see what could happen in a certain situation, e.g. if demand fell.

Quick Test 11

1. Decrease, as fewer employees will be required.
2. More information can be accessed.
3. They may feel technology is taking over their job.
4. The Freedom of Information Act.
5. The Data Protection Act.

Quick Test 12

1. Choosing the best option from a range of options.
2. Planning, controlling, co-ordinating, commanding, organising.
3. Strategic decisions are long-term decisions made by the senior management of an organisation. They are concerned with setting the overall direction of the organisation. Tactical decisions are decisions made to enable an organisation to achieve its strategic objectives. Tactical decisions are medium-term and made by middle management.

4. Finding cheaper suppliers of raw materials in order to cut costs, expanding the range of goods or services offered, seeking opportunities to sell goods or services in locations where they don't already, developing a new marketing campaign to raise awareness of the organisation's products.

Quick Test 13

1. As shown on page 34.
2. No quick decisions are made because time is given to gather information, time is given to think about and consider the range of options (alternatives) available, factors (internal and external) that may impact upon the decision are considered, the effectiveness and impact of each decision is considered during the evaluation stage.
3. It takes time to gather information and it may be difficult to obtain good quality information, the impact of each solution cannot be fully seen, it may be difficult to think of different solutions, instinct and gut reactions to situations are stifled.
4. S – Strengths, W – Weaknesses, O – Opportunities, T – Threats.

Quick Test 14

1. Any three from diagram on the 36.
2. Human (people) and financial (money).
3. External factors are those issues or constraints which may impact upon an organisation that are outwith its control. For example, law, the economy, advances in technology.

Quick Test 15

1. Marketing, Operations, Human Resources and Finance.
2. Grouping by departments that specialise in a particular product/service that the organisation sells.
3. Grouping by customer types.
4. Recruitment and selection of staff, arranging staff training, advising on employment terms and conditions, reviewing employee pay structures.
5. Processing requests for payment, paying employee wages, preparing budgets, preparing final accounts, carrying out financial analysis using ratios.

Answers to Quick Tests

Quick Test 16

1. It is a diagram of an organisation's structure.
2. A manager with a wide span of control has many subordinates whereas a manager with a narrow span of control has few subordinates.
3. The way instructions are passed down through an organisation.
4. To enable people to come together to work on specific purposes, e.g. a project or task.
5. The authority to make decisions has been delegated.

Quick Test 17

1. Communication takes place in ways that are not seen by looking at the formal organisation structure.
2. Everything to do with the organisation including its values, emotions, beliefs and language used. It is also to do with the attitude and behaviours that members of the organisation adopt.
3. Removing layers of management to create a flatter structure.
4. Quicker communication, quicker decision making, quicker response to changing market conditions, staff empowerment.
5. Getting another organisation to carry out an activity on the organisation's behalf.

Quick Test 18

1. Product life cycle shows the stages a product will go through in its life.
2. Development, introduction, growth, maturity, decline.
3. It shows the range of products sold by a business.
4. Brand loyalty, associated with quality, easily recognisable, new products can be introduced more easily, higher prices can be charged.
5. Little advertising required, associated with value for money, manufactured by other companies.

Quick Test 19

1. Price is how much is charged for a product.
2. Any two from the bullet points on page 50.
3. Low price is set when a product enters the market.
4. Selling a product at a loss (lower than what is costs to make).
5. Unique and exclusiveness commands a higher price.

Quick Test 20

1. The route a product takes from being manufactured to get to the customer.
2. A retailer distributes products to customers in small quantities.
3. A wholesaler buys in bulk from a manufacturer and sells smaller quantities to retailers.
4. Internet selling, direct mail and mail order.
5. Customer can choose when and where to order and can do it 24/7 from the convenience of their own home or workplace.

Quick Test 21

1. It is the different methods an organisation uses to make customers aware that a product exists and also the ways they are encouraged to buy it. It includes advertising, promotions and public relations.
2. Their computer system could crash, they could have problems with making a secure payment or they might find it hard to navigate their way around the website.
3. Famous celebrities are used to promote an organisation and its products.
4. Point of sale materials, sale or return, staff training, dealer loaders.
5. It is the term used to create positive relationships between the organisation and the general public.
6. It is usually a statement to the press that communicates the activities within the organisation.

Quick Test 22

1. Desk and field.
2. Desk research looks at secondary information and field research involves collecting primary (new) information for specific purposes.
3. Postal survey, telephone survey, personal interview.
4. A discussion between a selected number of people and researcher on certain things.
5. A sample is a selected group of people from the whole population who have been asked to take part in something, e.g. a survey.

Quick Test 23

1. The role of operations is to transform inputs into outputs. It is concerned with making goods and services.
2. Operations is important as it is a core business activity. Products must be produced of a quality that will generate revenue and keep wastage low.

3. The factors/issues to be considered when choosing a supplier and the quantity of raw materials to be purchased.
4. Because production could stop and customer orders might not be met on time if the supplier was not reliable.

Quick Test 24

1. Raw materials, work in progress and finished goods.
2. The best quantity of stock at any one time.
3. Centralisation is where stock is stored in one central location whereas decentralisation is where stock is stored in more than one location.
4. Distribution mix identifies factors that need to be considered when deciding how to get the product to the customer.

Quick Test 25

1. Job, batch and flow.
2. Flow.
3. Machines as well as some degree of labour are used in the production process.
4. Machinery.

Quick Test 26

1. Quality control involves checking the finished product whereas quality assurance involves checking the product at various stages of the production process.
2. It involves members of the organisation meeting regularly to discuss quality issues and then attempting to find ways to solve these.
3. Improves its name/image, provides competitive advantage.

Quick Test 27

1. Any three from the diagram on page 78.
2. Relationship between organisation/supplier may be become damaged. Credit rating could be affected.
3. Budget.
4. 50%
5. Definitely not!

Quick Test 28

1. Sole trader and partnership
2. Fixed Assets are items owned that will last for over a year, whereas Current Assets are items owned that will be used up within a year.
3. Current Assets less Current Liabilities.
4. It will decrease.
5. It will increase.

Quick Test 29

1. So that bills and day-to-day expenses can be paid for.
2. Any two reasons from list at top of page 82.
3. A forecast of the inflows (receipts) and outflows (payments) of cash over a period of time.
4. A negative closing cash balance.

Quick Test 30

1. How able it is to pay its short-term debts.
2. To see if they should be given a pay rise, to understand decision making and to see if jobs are secure.
3. Ratios.
4. It has assets, has a strong brand name, has a large/loyal customer base.
5. To decide whether to issue a loan or increase an overdraft.

Quick Test 31

1. To compare their performance from one year to the next or against competitors.
2. How profitable the organisation is. They are used to analyse the organisation's expenses, cost of stock and the selling price.
3. $\frac{\text{Net Profit}}{\text{Capital Employed}} \times 100 = \_\_\_\%$
4. Stock is included in the current ratio calculation whereas it is not in the acid test ratio.

Quick Test 32

1. Bank overdraft, trade credit, government grant.
2. An item is purchased and a deposit paid with the remaining balance being paid over time in instalments. The item belongs to the seller when all payments are made.
3. Venture capitalist.
4. Share issue.

Quick Test 33

1. Facilitator, Auditor, Consultancy, Executive and Service.
2. Any two from the diagram on page 93.
3. It is important so that the organisation keeps up with changing employment patterns and can take appropriate action to meet future requirements.
4. When a person is employed on a casual basis for only a short period of time.

Answers to Quick Tests

Quick Test 34

1. Recruitment involves encouraging people to apply for a job vacancy.
2. Conducting a job analysis.
3. At least two.
4. Staff notice board, e-mail.
5. People with new ideas can be brought into the organisation or large quantities of applications can be received.

Quick Test 35

1. A written report on an applicant's suitability for a job usually by an existing or previous employer.
2. Attainment, psychometric, intelligence, medical and aptitude.
3. An application form is designed and issued by the organisation with specific questions whereas a CV is designed by the applicant and contains information that they choose to disclose.
4. Choosing from the applications received those to invite to the next stage of the selection process.

Quick Test 36

1. Induction training.
2. On-the-job training takes place within their own place of work whereas off-the-job training takes place outwith the organisation by a specialist trainer.
3. Coaching, presentations, job rotation, demonstrations and role plays.
4. Identify strengths and development needs (opportunities for training).

Quick Test 37

1. Because employees are fundamental to an organisation achieving its objectives.
2. A trade union represents employees on employment-related issues.
3. Sit in, strike, work to rule, boycott, overtime ban, go slow.
4. A complaint regarding a work-related issue made by an employee to their employer.